T0312968

JUST PEACHY

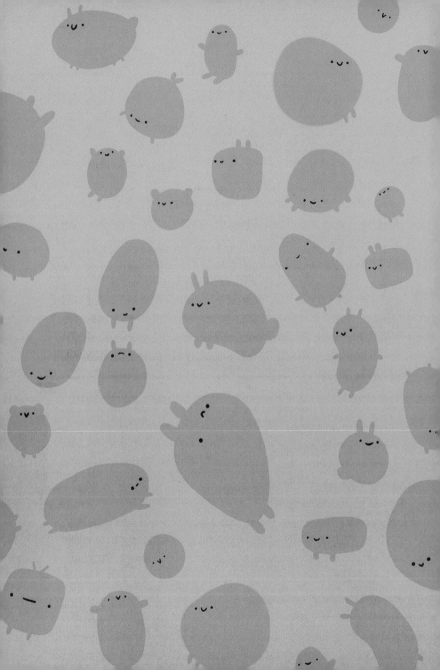

JUST PEACHY

Comics about Depression, Anxiety, Love, and Finding the Humor in Being Sad

by Holly Chisholm

Skyhorse Publishing

Introduction 1

Depression
15

Anxiety
45

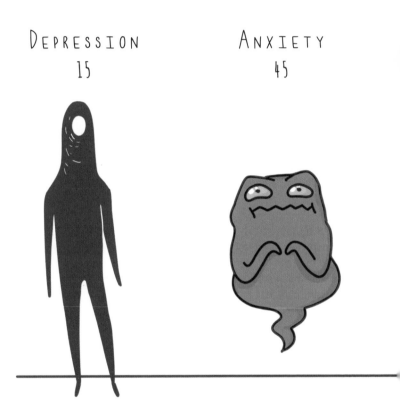

Love and
Relationships
75

Growth
99

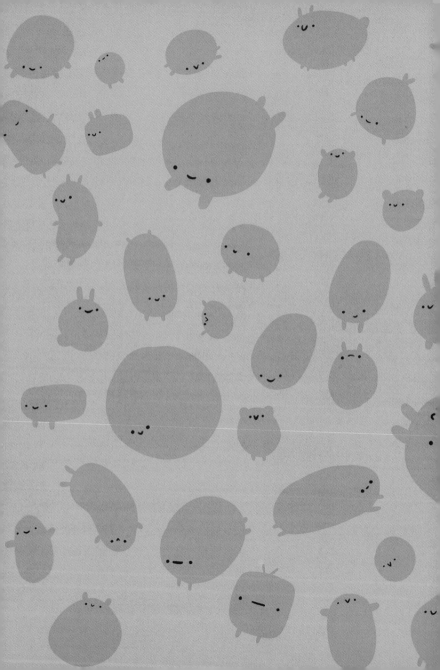

INTRODUCTION

I WAS DIAGNOSED WITH DEPRESSION IN DECEMBER OF 2016.

THE UNUSUAL COLD AND RAIN IN SOUTHERN CALIFORNIA SEEMED FITTING.

I began taking medication. Bupropion—100mg.

I couldn't stay up past 9:00 p.m. I felt sleepy all day. I broke out in hives.

I stopped taking Bupropion.

I cried for three days straight.

It was a new year.

I began seeing a therapist.

She told me to journal. She said I probably had ADHD, too. She referred me to a psychiatrist.

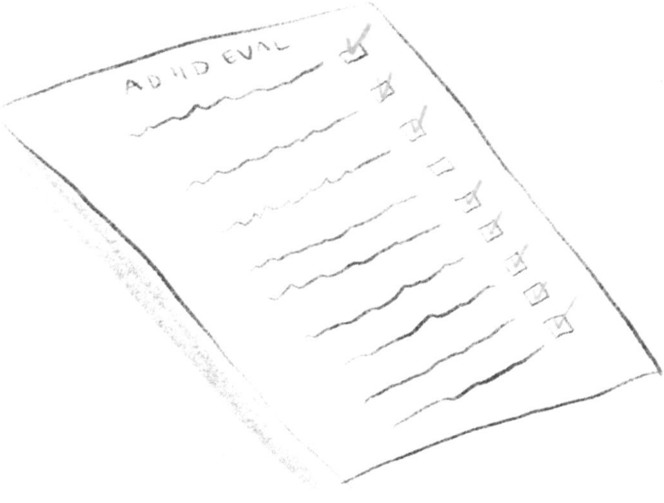
ADHD EVAL

The psychiatrist prescribed me Prozac, 10mg.

He prescribed me the lowest dose of Ritalin.

He prescribed me Lorazepam in case I had an anxiety attack.

To balance, I quit smoking my occasional cigarette and started nicotine patches to wean off.

I could focus at work suddenly.

I could focus on how my teeth felt too tight.

I could focus on the dark shadows in my room when
I couldn't sleep at 3:00 a.m.

I could focus on the walls crawling when I took
the Lorazepam to calm down.

I could focus on the new and peculiar thought of
wanting to die.

WHEN I HAD MY THIRD ANXIETY ATTACK IN A MONTH, SILENTLY CRYING ON THE BATHROOM FLOOR AT WORK, I STOPPED TAKING THE RITALIN.

OF COURSE, I KEPT A FEW, JUST IN CASE.

THE PSYCHIATRIST SAID THAT PEOPLE WITH ADHD DRINK LOTS OF COFFEE AS A WAY TO SELF-MEDICATE.

I HAVE LOVED COFFEE MOST OF MY ADULT LIFE.

I LOVE COFFEE A LITTLE LESS NOW.

My therapist told me to journal again.

I tried. My writing sounded whiny.

My teeth still felt too tight. My chest still felt full of gravity and bad fluorescent lighting.

"I went to school for art. Maybe I will draw my feelings instead."

So, I did.

Sometimes it helped. Sometimes I had to force myself to do it. Sometimes it was the only thing I could think of to do when my breaths were too short and my eyes were too wet.
I drew almost every day.

Spring turned to summer, and my depression seemed less fitting than it had in December.

It was hot. I felt like I was squeezing into a dress two sizes too small. My job was trying to forcibly zip up the back of it.

FIT. FIT. FIT!

I quit.

My psychiatrist prescribed me Lamictal.

"It treats bipolar disorder and seizures, but it should also help with your mood swings. There can be really bad side effects on your skin, but they would show up within 24 hours."

I looked up pictures of people's skin sloughing off like bark peeling off a tree.

I was terrified.

I took two tablets for a total of 50mg.

My skin didn't peel off.

"It will take about 6 weeks to start working."

One green, two white. One green, two white.
One green, two white.

I GOT A NEW (LESS STRESSFUL) JOB.

I GOT A NEW BOYFRIEND: THE GOOD KIND WHO DOESN'T
SCREAM AT YOU IN PUBLIC.

I WENT TO THE GYM FOR THE FIRST TIME IN
SIX MONTHS.

I DREW.

THINGS STARTED TO FEEL EVEN.

I was diagnosed with depression in December, of 2016.

Now I take no greens, three whites, and a variety of vitamins. I drastically reduced drinking alcohol. I meditate more.

I am able to sit in the window seat of a plane without crying.

Some days are bad, but never as bad as they were.

And I still draw. And I feel better when people tell me they have bad days too, and on my bad days they remind me it will get better.

Because it WILL get better. Even if it's only 10% better. Even if the drawing isn't very good. Even if the page gets tears on it and I have to start over. Even if some days I still feel like a small melon baller is slowly scooping out parts of my chest.

At least I hope it will.

THERE'S ONLY ONE WAY TO FIND OUT.

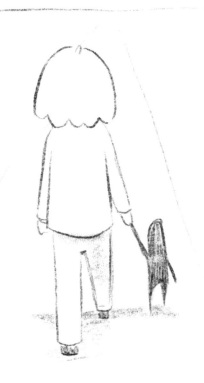

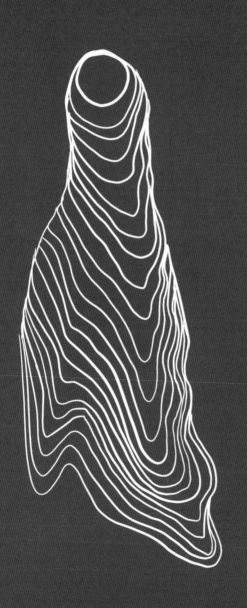

DEPRESSION

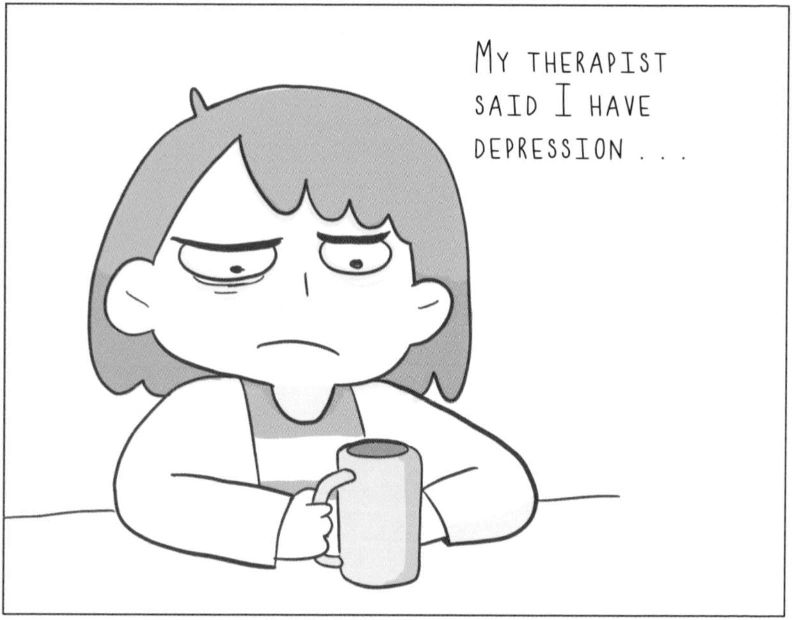
MY THERAPIST SAID I HAVE DEPRESSION . . .

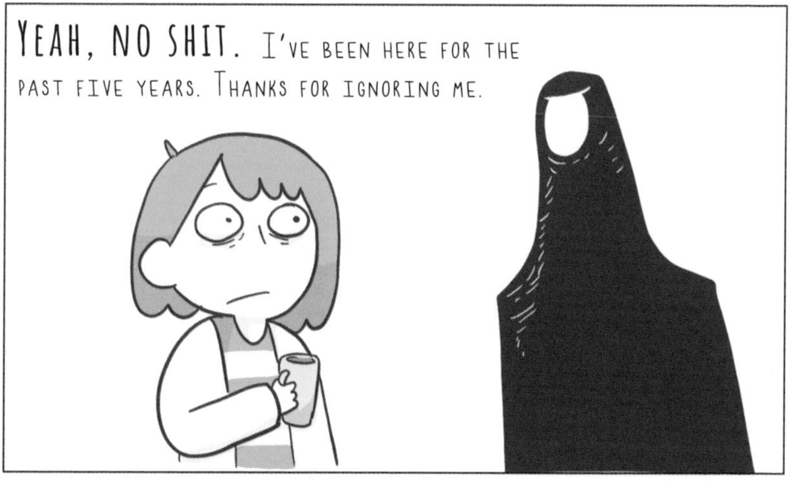
YEAH, NO SHIT. I'VE BEEN HERE FOR THE PAST FIVE YEARS. THANKS FOR IGNORING ME.

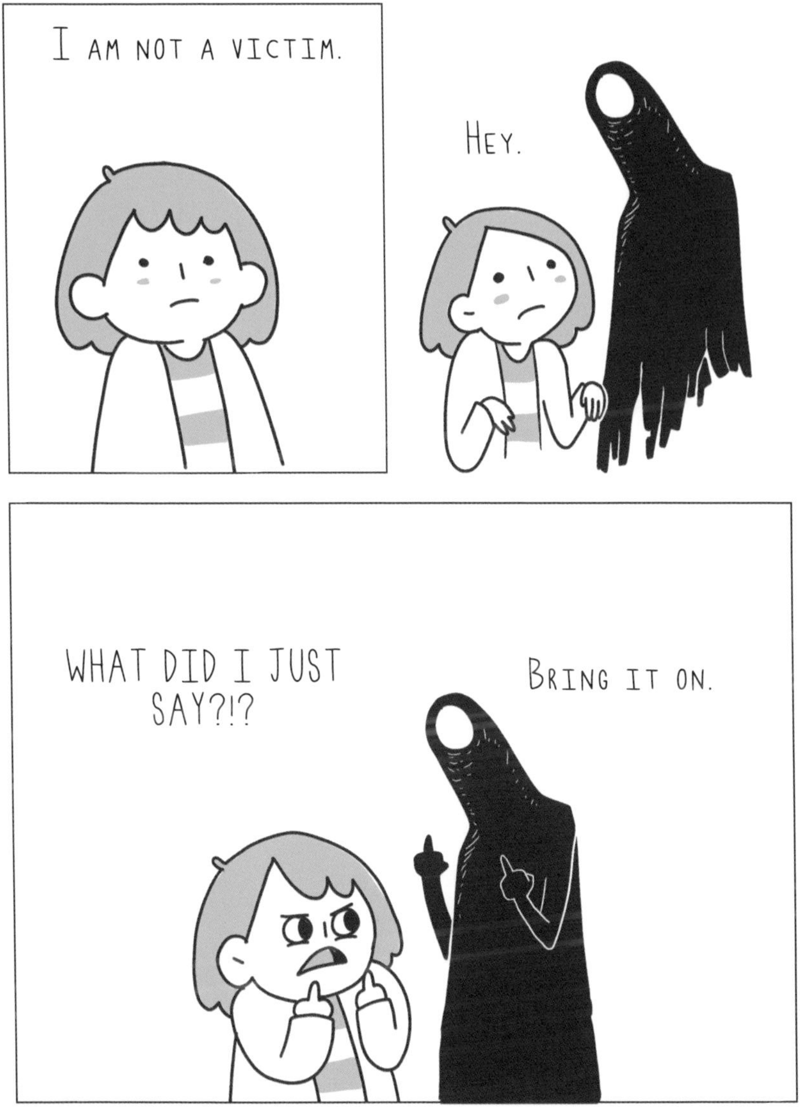
I AM NOT A VICTIM.
HEY.
WHAT DID I JUST SAY?!?
BRING IT ON.

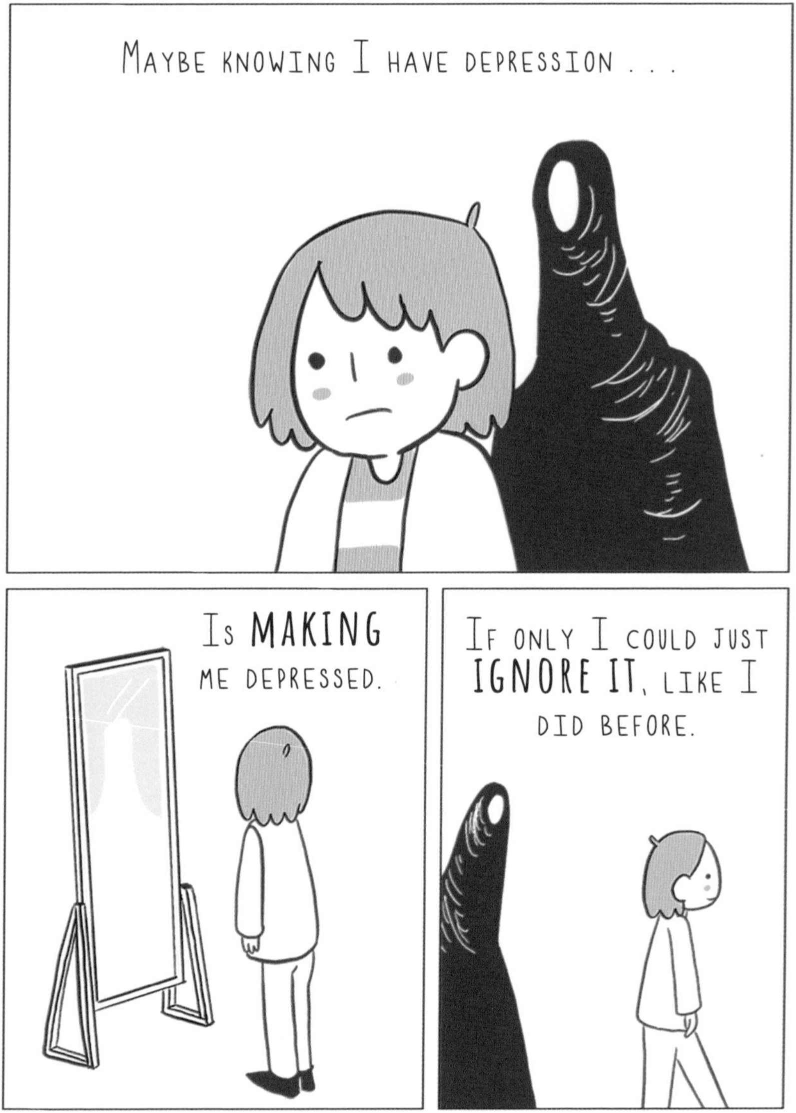
MAYBE KNOWING I HAVE DEPRESSION . . .
IS MAKING ME DEPRESSED.
IF ONLY I COULD JUST IGNORE IT, LIKE I DID BEFORE.

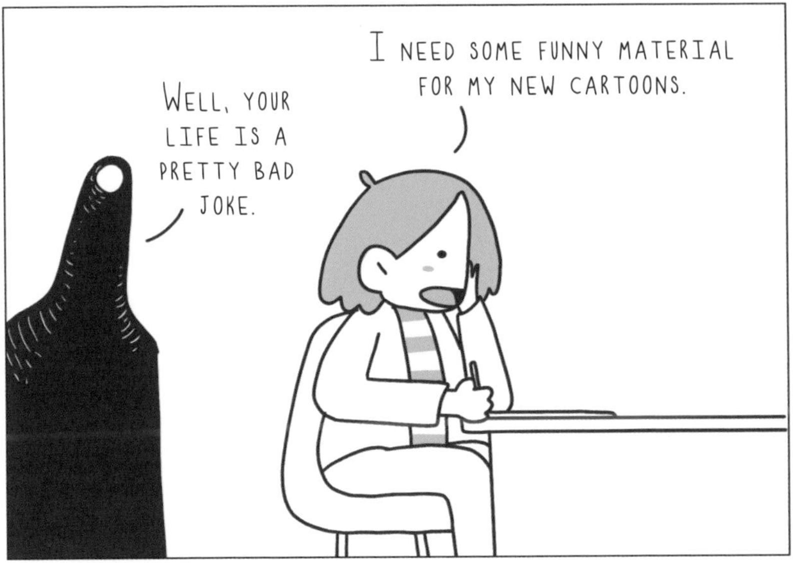
I NEED SOME FUNNY MATERIAL FOR MY NEW CARTOONS.
WELL, YOUR LIFE IS A PRETTY BAD JOKE.

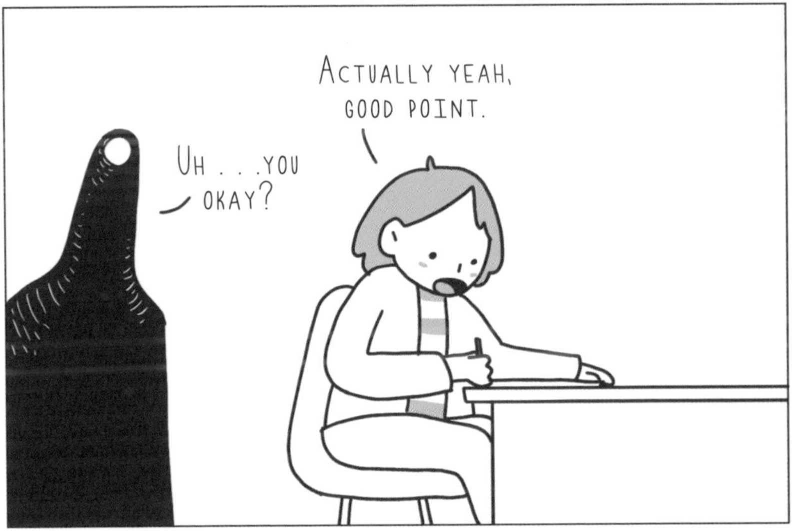
ACTUALLY YEAH, GOOD POINT.
UH . . .YOU OKAY?

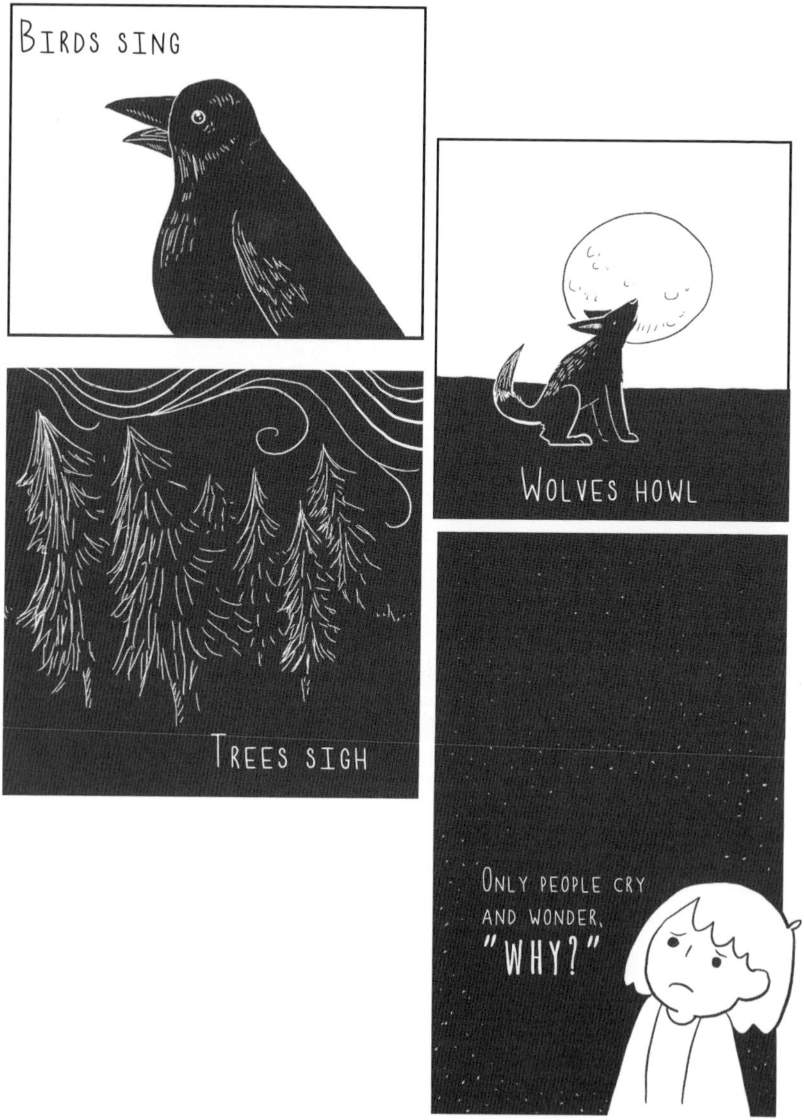
BIRDS SING
TREES SIGH
WOLVES HOWL
ONLY PEOPLE CRY
AND WONDER,
"WHY?"

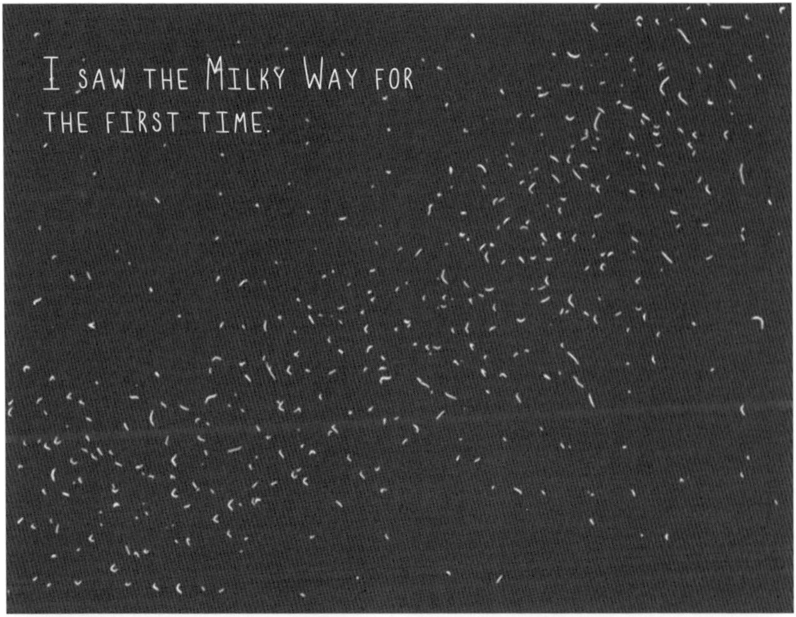
I SAW THE MILKY WAY FOR THE FIRST TIME.

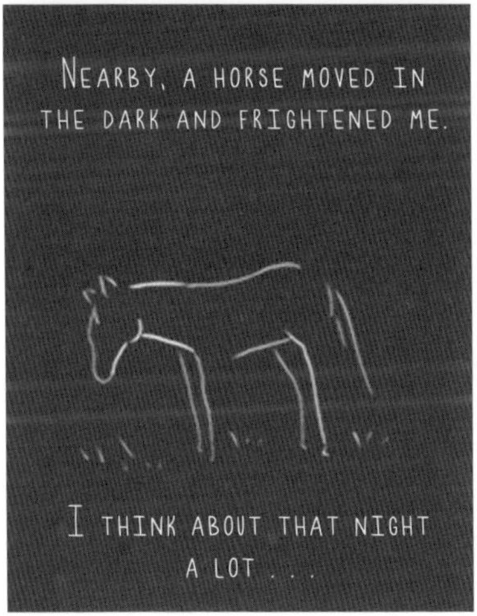
NEARBY, A HORSE MOVED IN THE DARK AND FRIGHTENED ME.
I THINK ABOUT THAT NIGHT A LOT . . .

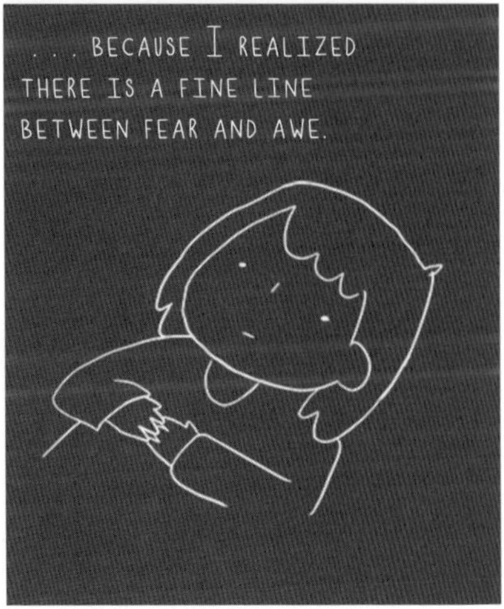
. . . BECAUSE I REALIZED THERE IS A FINE LINE BETWEEN FEAR AND AWE.

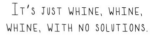
PEOPLE WHO COMPLAIN ARE **SO ANNOYING.**

IT'S JUST WHINE, WHINE, WHINE, WITH NO SOLUTIONS.

WHY ARE PEOPLE LIKE THAT? WHY CAN'T THEY JUST **GET OVER IT?**

WELL, MAYBE YOU SHOULD TRY TO DO SOMETHING ABOUT IT?

WHY WOULD I?

Go outside!

Go outside!

Go outside!

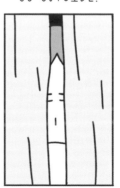

Go outside . . .

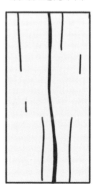

PARTY NOISES
DRUNK PEOPLE
HAHA
MY NEIGHBORS SUCK!
I LOVE YOU GUYS!
HEHE
AWWW!
I WISH THEY WOULD INVITE ME OVER.

The depressed introvert

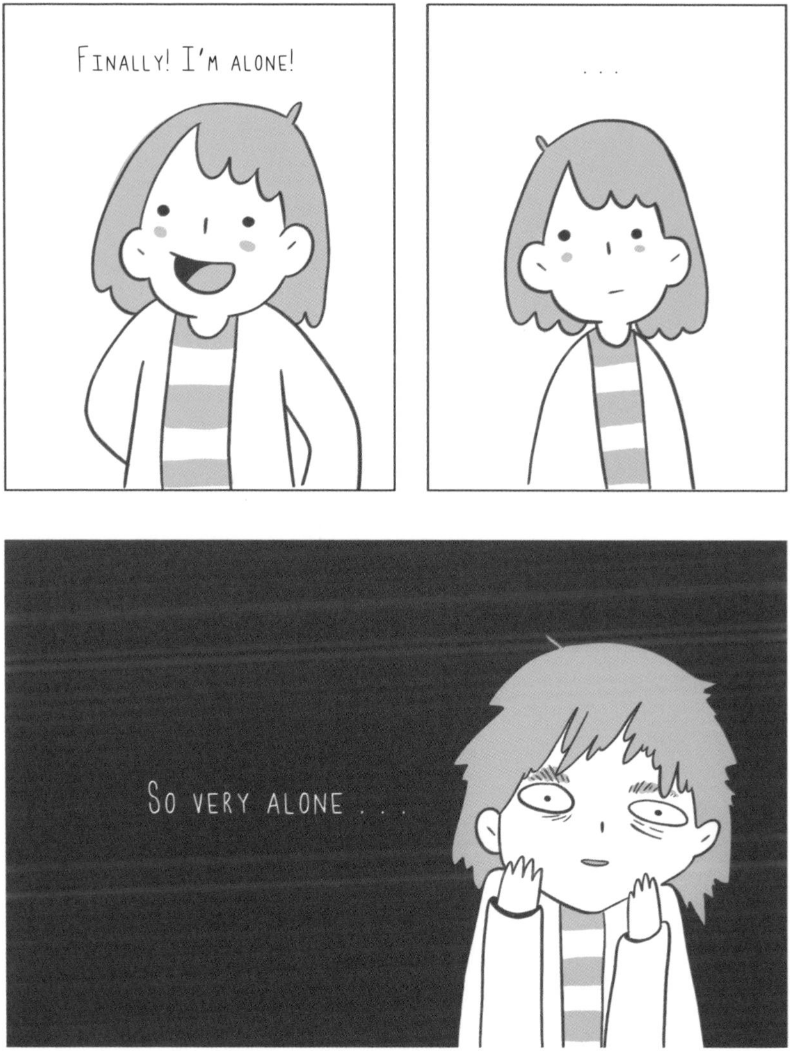
Finally! I'm alone!
. . .
So very alone . . .

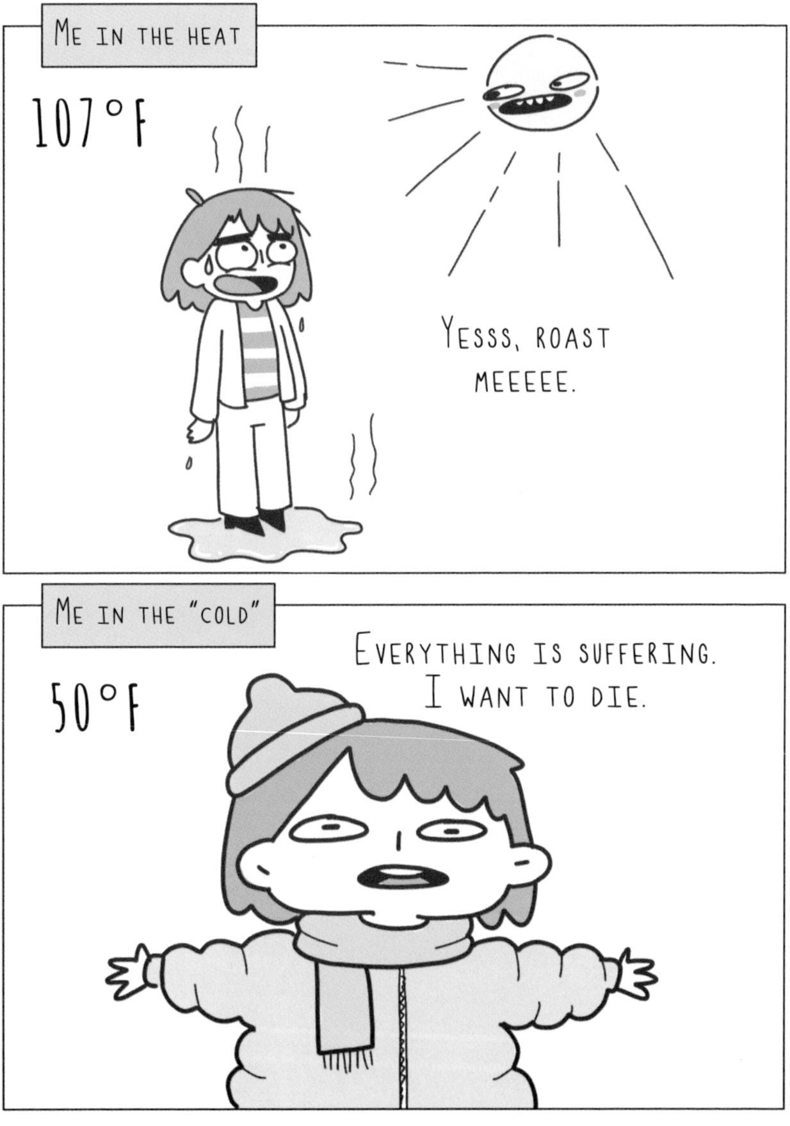
Me in the heat
107°F
Yesss, roast
meeeeee.
Me in the "cold"
50°F
Everything is suffering.
I want to die.

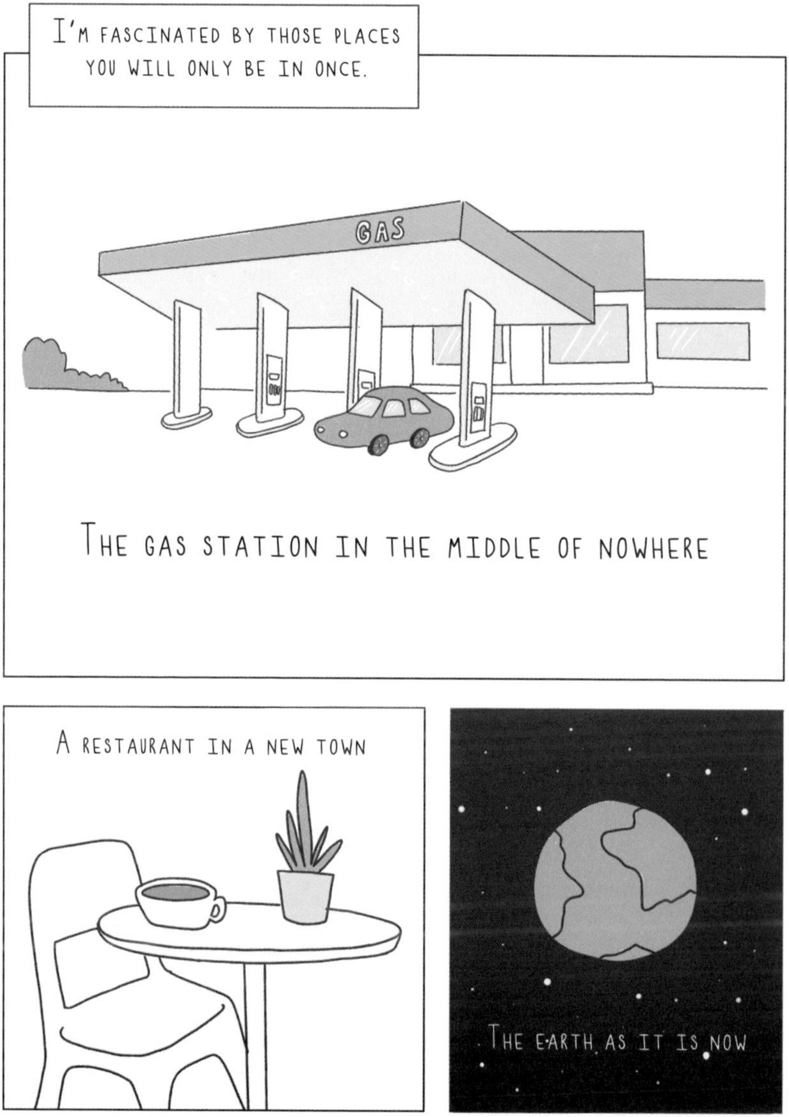
I'M FASCINATED BY THOSE PLACES YOU WILL ONLY BE IN ONCE.
GAS
THE GAS STATION IN THE MIDDLE OF NOWHERE
A RESTAURANT IN A NEW TOWN
THE EARTH AS IT IS NOW

Consequences of not trying

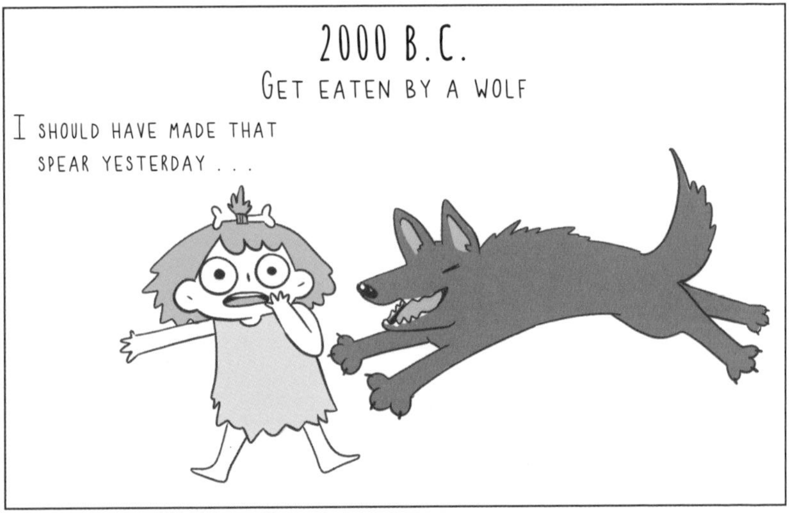
2000 B.C.
Get eaten by a wolf
I should have made that spear yesterday . . .

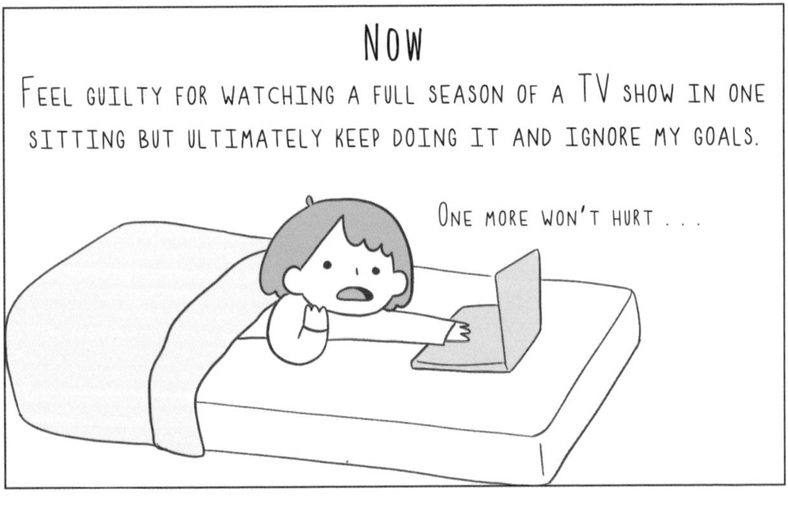
Now
Feel guilty for watching a full season of a TV show in one sitting but ultimately keep doing it and ignore my goals.
One more won't hurt . . .

I USUALLY TRY TO SEPARATE MY THOUGHTS.

NEGATIVE thoughts about MYSELF →

THOUGHTS I SHARE WITH OTHERS

BUT EVERY ONCE IN A WHILE,

I PROJECT MY INSECURITIES ONTO OTHER PEOPLE.

WHEN I SEE HOW MUCH IT HURTS THEM, I WONDER WHY I LET MYSELF BE SO MEAN TO ME.

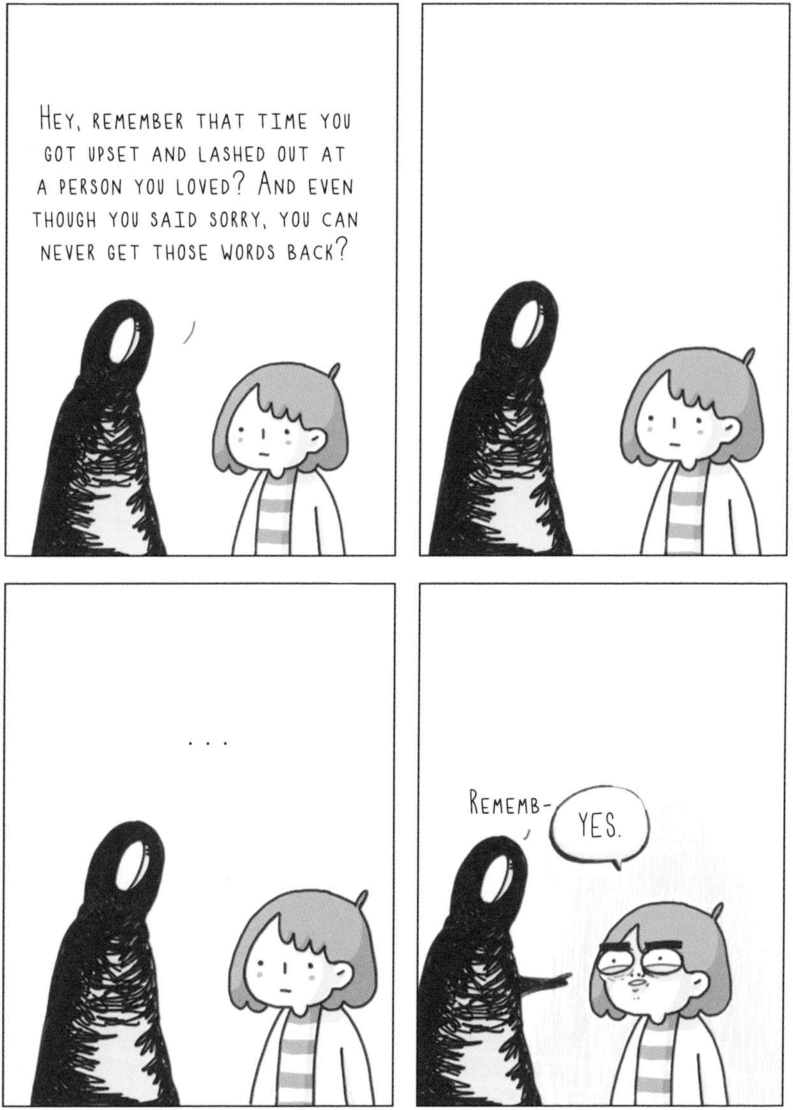
HEY, REMEMBER THAT TIME YOU GOT UPSET AND LASHED OUT AT A PERSON YOU LOVED? AND EVEN THOUGH YOU SAID SORRY, YOU CAN NEVER GET THOSE WORDS BACK?
...
REMEMB-
YES.

THE HARDEST PART OF GROWING UP IS
APOLOGIZING BUT KNOWING THAT SAYING
SORRY MIGHT NOT FIX WHAT YOU DID.

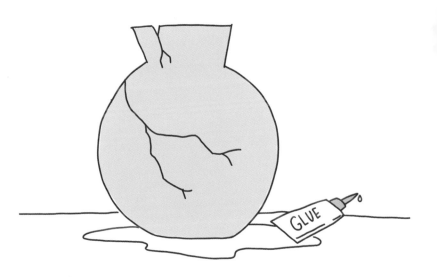

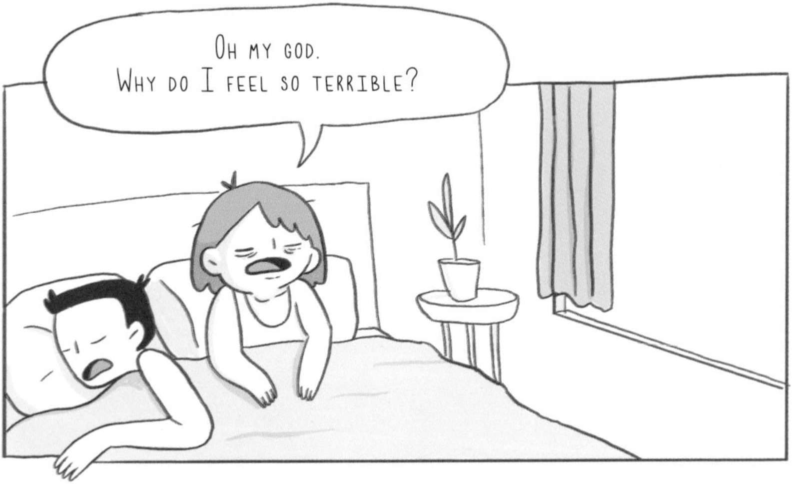
OH MY GOD.
WHY DO I FEEL SO TERRIBLE?

LITERALLY YESTERDAY . . .

1. OVERSLEPT

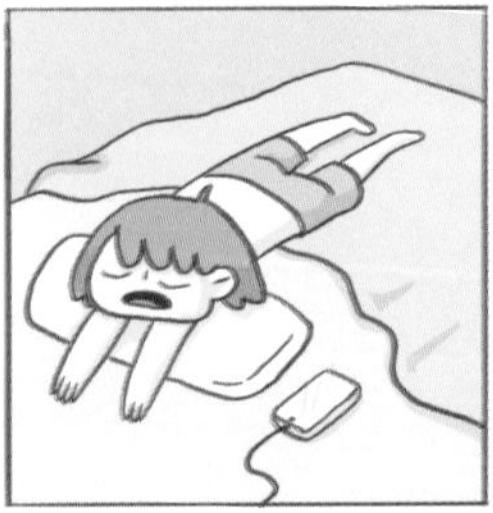

2. ATE LIKE GARBAGE

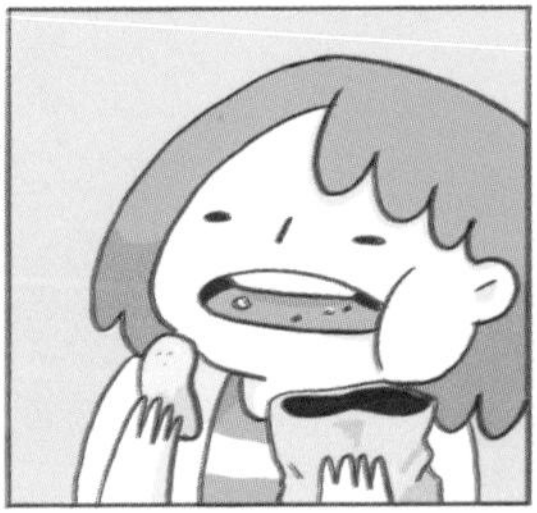

3. DRANK WAY TOO MUCH

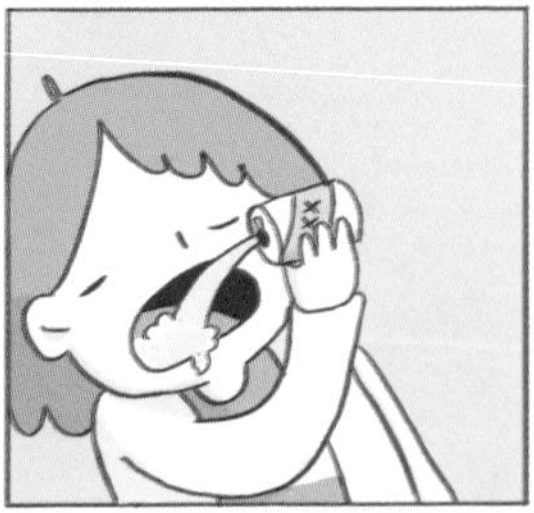

ME ON THREE HOURS OF SLEEP

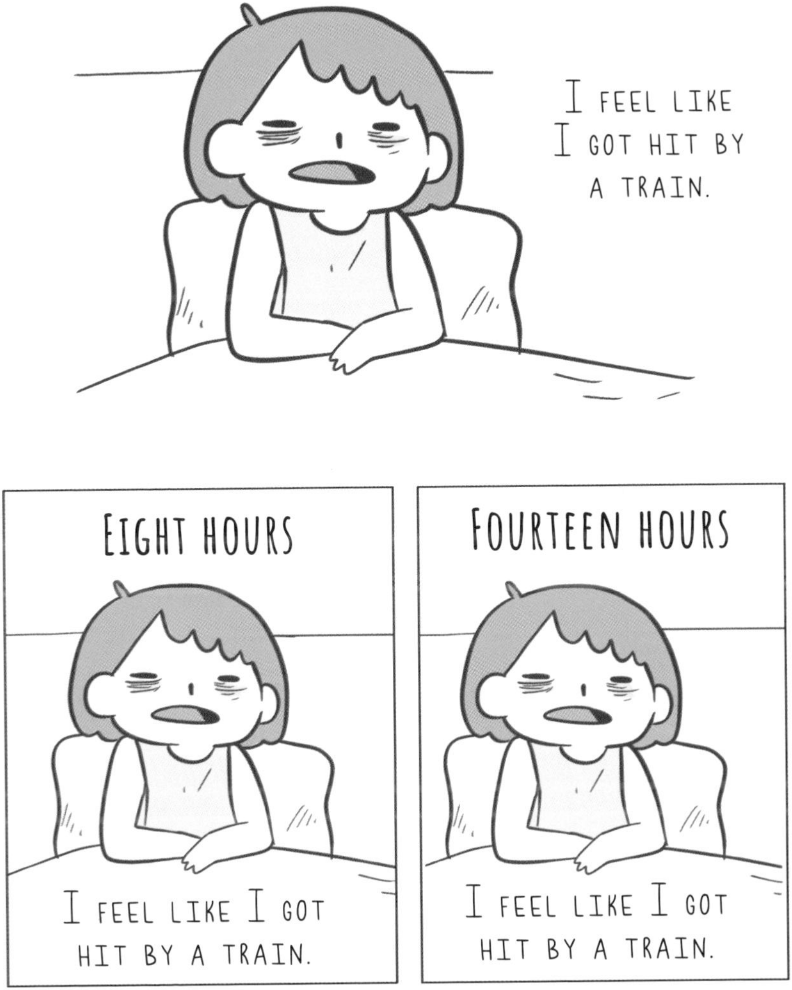

I FEEL LIKE I GOT HIT BY A TRAIN.
EIGHT HOURS
I FEEL LIKE I GOT HIT BY A TRAIN.
FOURTEEN HOURS
I FEEL LIKE I GOT HIT BY A TRAIN.

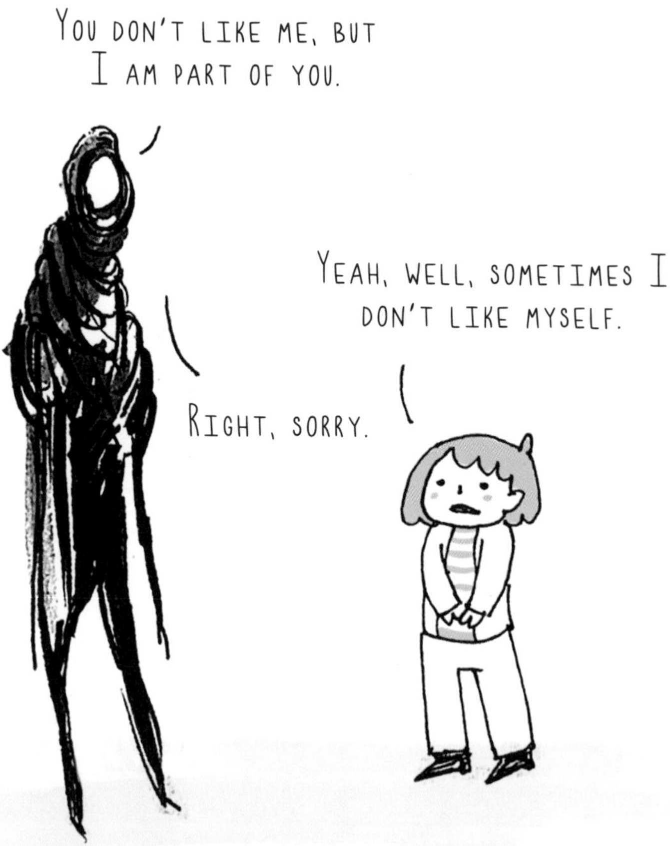
YOU DON'T LIKE ME, BUT I AM PART OF YOU.
YEAH, WELL, SOMETIMES I DON'T LIKE MYSELF.
RIGHT, SORRY.

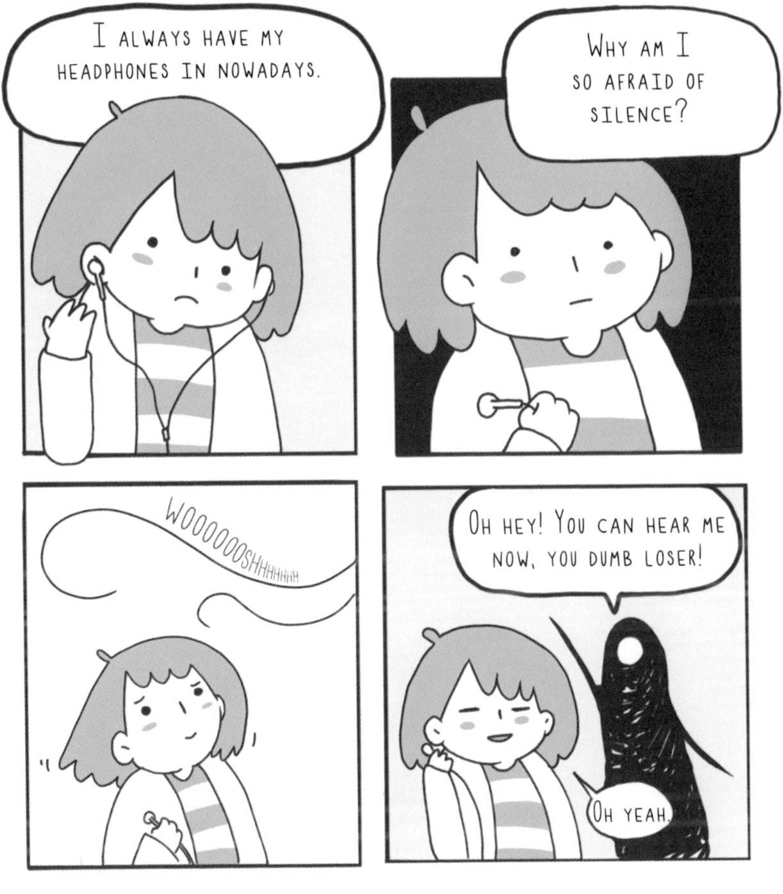
I ALWAYS HAVE MY HEADPHONES IN NOWADAYS.
WHY AM I SO AFRAID OF SILENCE?
WOOOOOOOSHHHHHHH
OH HEY! YOU CAN HEAR ME NOW, YOU DUMB LOSER!
OH YEAH.

SOMETIMES I SEE A WOMAN SO BEAUTIFUL I WONDER HOW WE ARE EVEN THE SAME SPECIES.

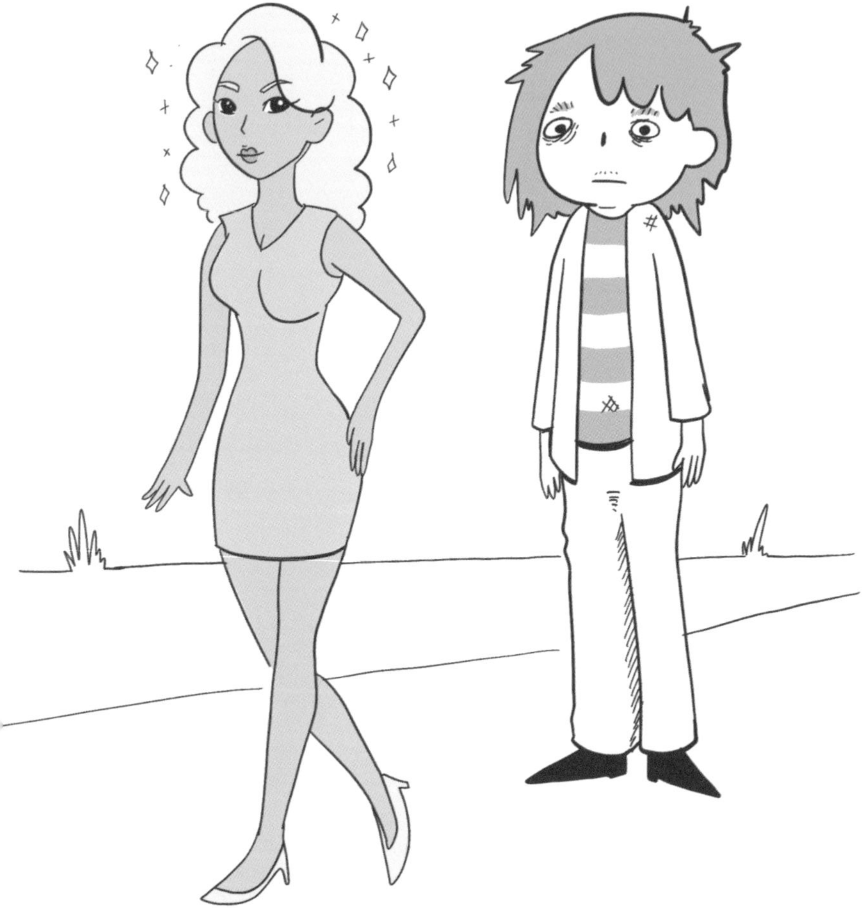

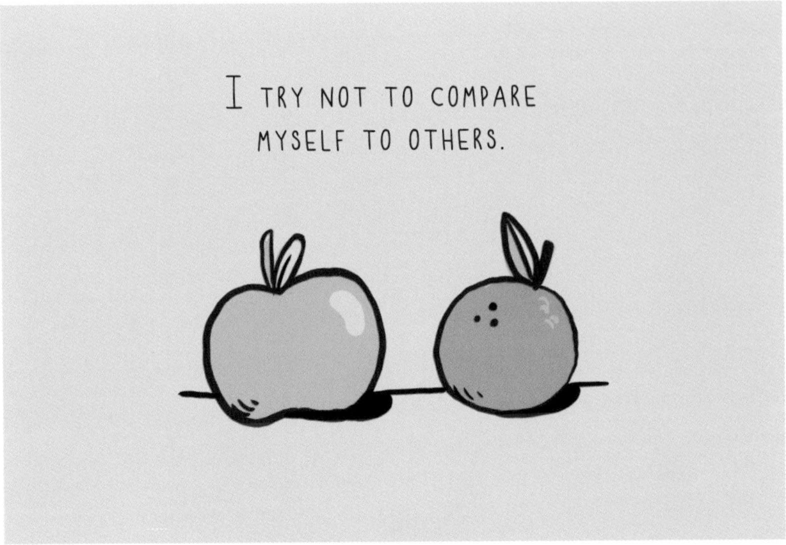
I TRY NOT TO COMPARE
MYSELF TO OTHERS.

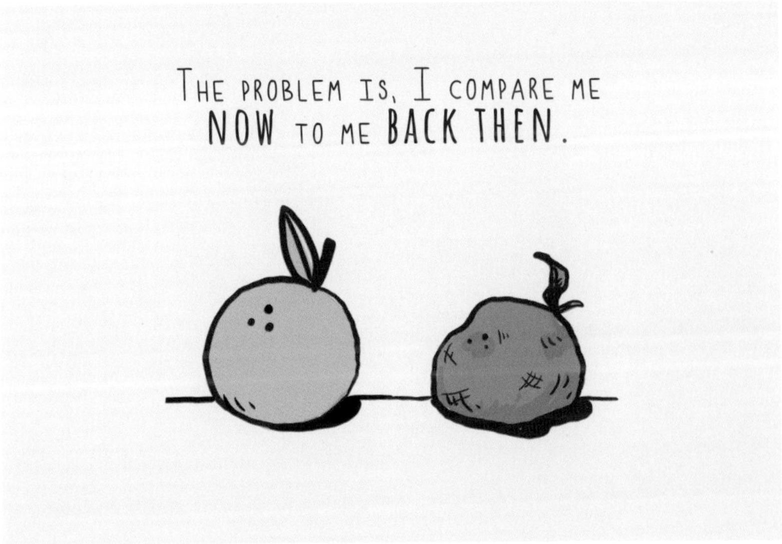
THE PROBLEM IS, I COMPARE ME
NOW TO ME BACK THEN.

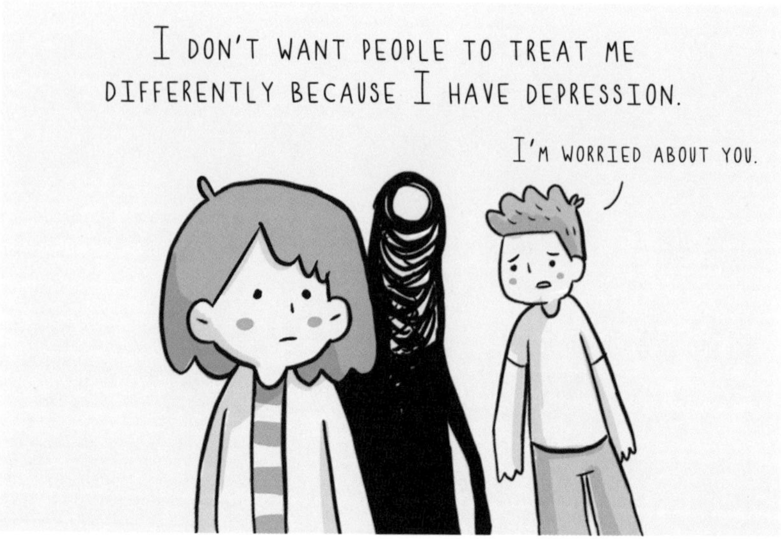
I DON'T WANT PEOPLE TO TREAT ME DIFFERENTLY BECAUSE I HAVE DEPRESSION.
I'M WORRIED ABOUT YOU.

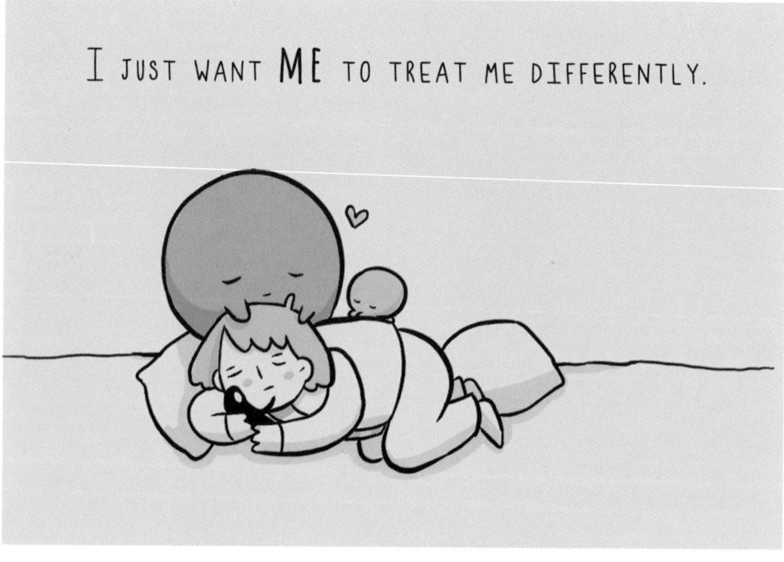
I JUST WANT ME TO TREAT ME DIFFERENTLY.

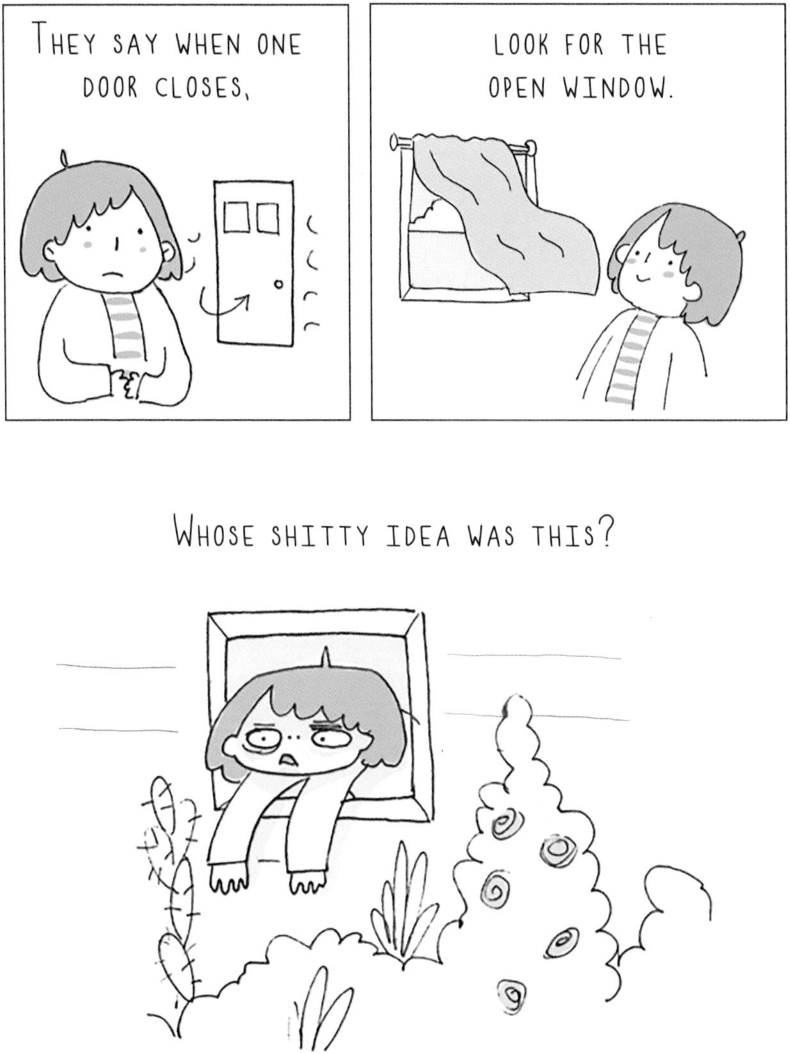
THEY SAY WHEN ONE DOOR CLOSES,
LOOK FOR THE OPEN WINDOW.
WHOSE SHITTY IDEA WAS THIS?

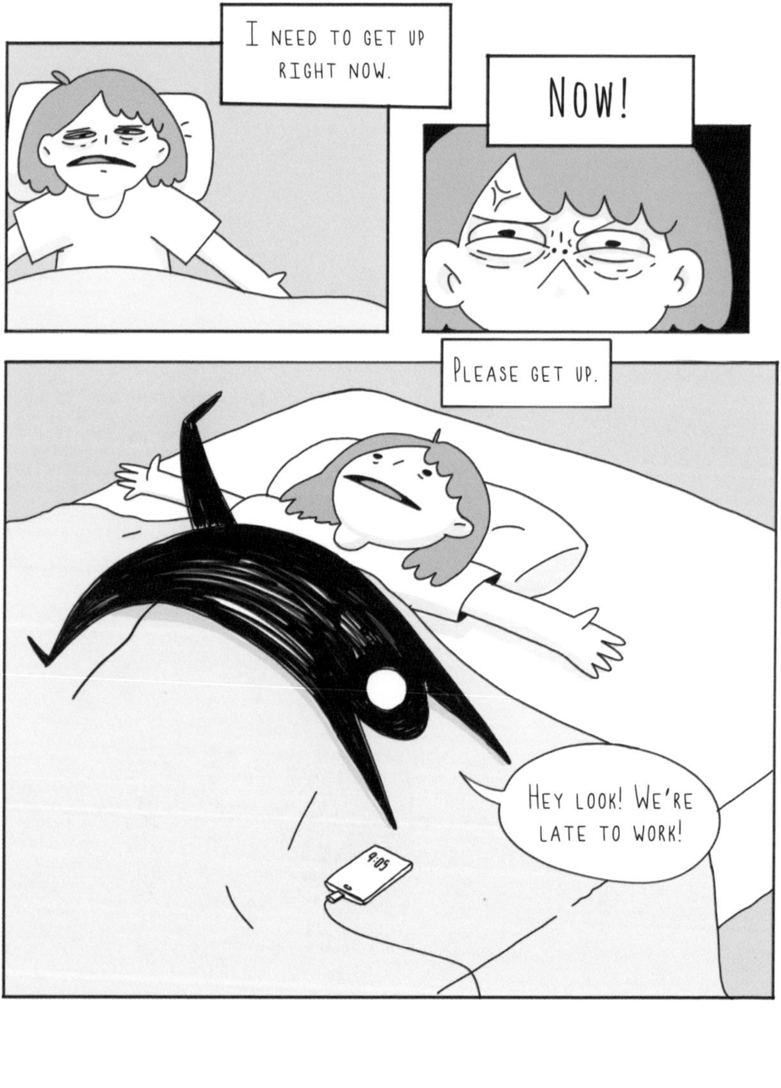
I NEED TO GET UP RIGHT NOW.
NOW!
PLEASE GET UP.
HEY LOOK! WE'RE LATE TO WORK!
9:05

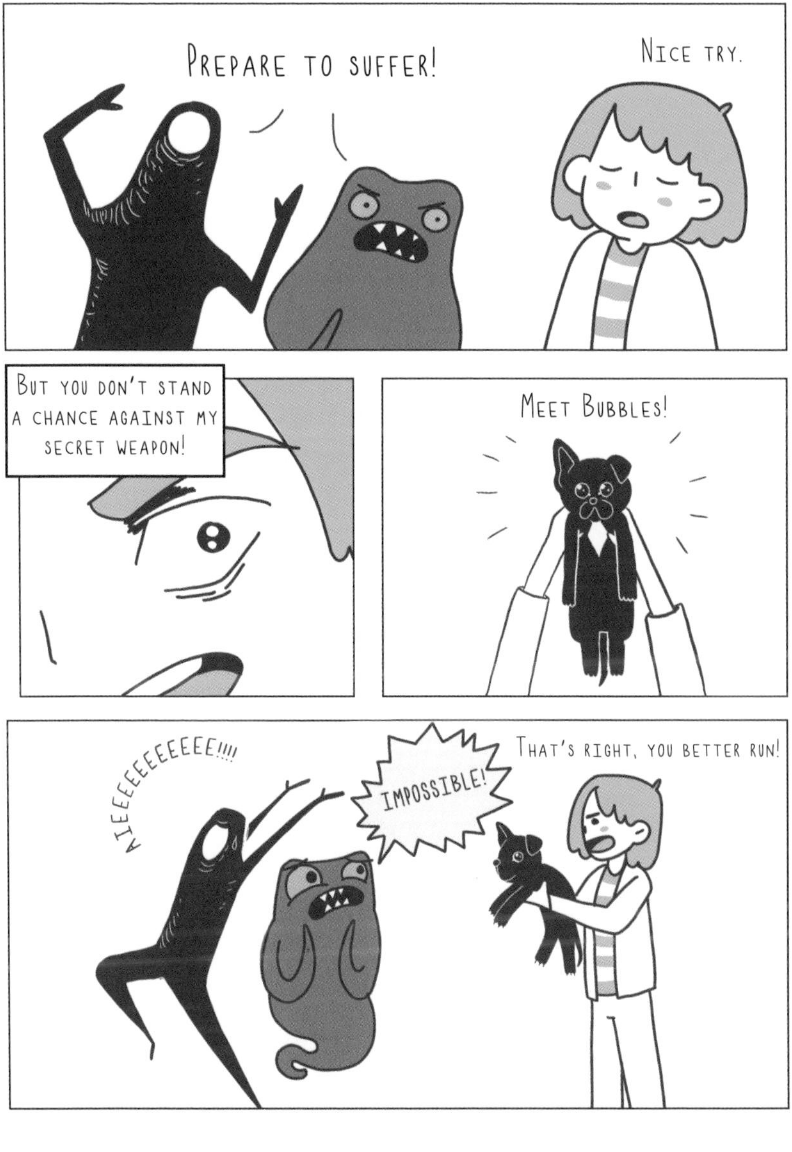
PREPARE TO SUFFER!
NICE TRY.
BUT YOU DON'T STAND A CHANCE AGAINST MY SECRET WEAPON!
MEET BUBBLES!
AIEEEEEEEEEEE!!!!
IMPOSSIBLE!
THAT'S RIGHT, YOU BETTER RUN!

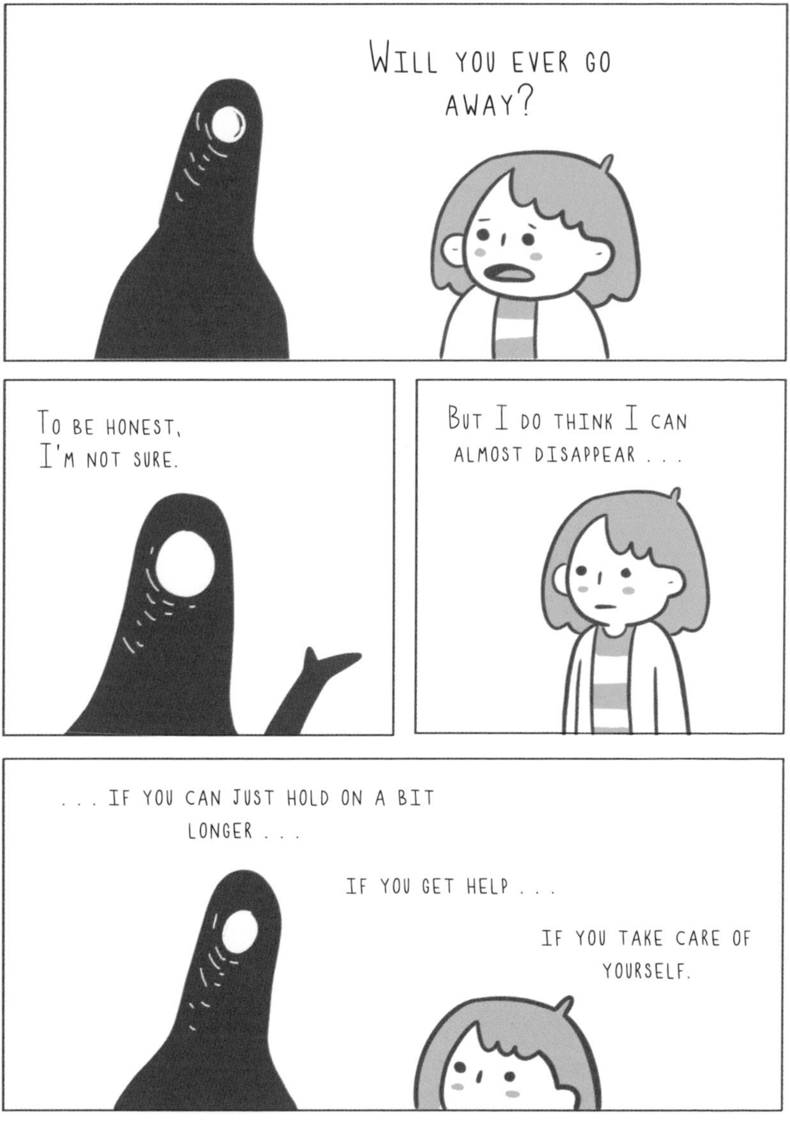

WILL YOU EVER GO AWAY?
TO BE HONEST, I'M NOT SURE.
BUT I DO THINK I CAN ALMOST DISAPPEAR . . .
. . . IF YOU CAN JUST HOLD ON A BIT LONGER . . .
IF YOU GET HELP . . .
IF YOU TAKE CARE OF YOURSELF.

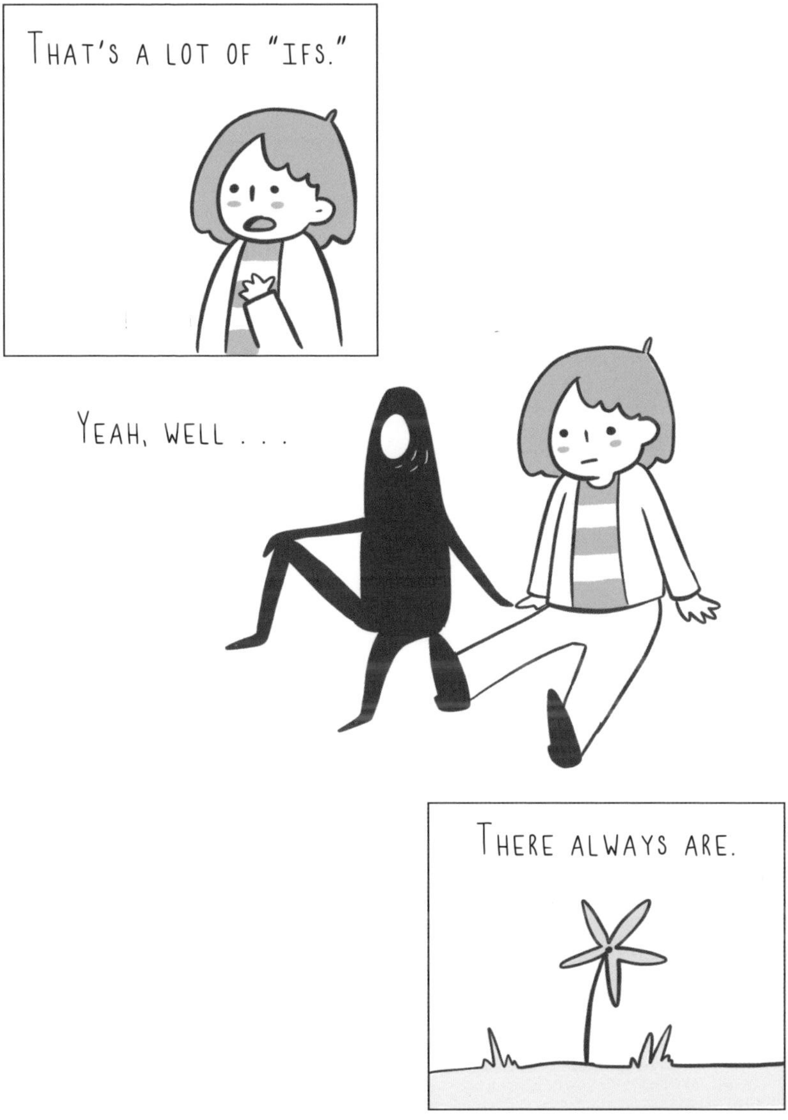
That's a lot of "ifs."
Yeah, well . . .
There always are.

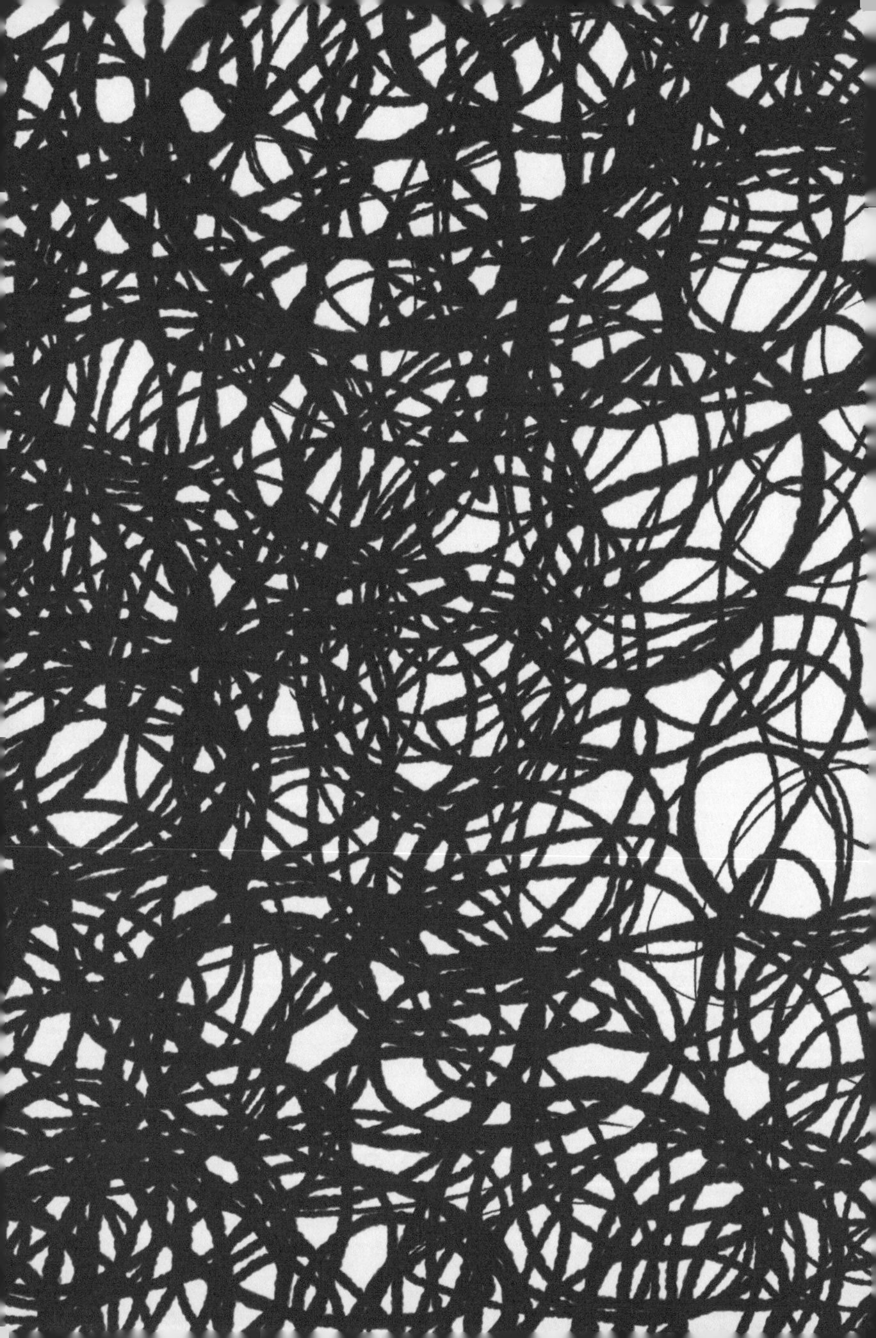

ANXIETY

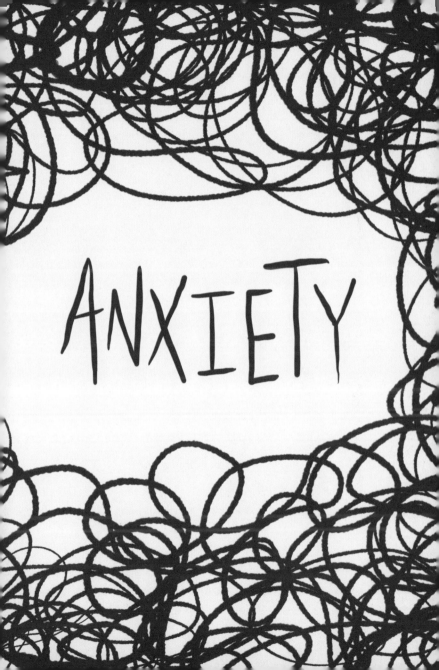

EEEEEEEEEEEEEEEEEEEEEEEEEEEEE
EEEEEEEEEEEEE
EEEEEEEEEEEEEE
MMMMMMMMMMMM
OOOOOOOOOOOOOOOO
OOOOOOTTTT
IIIOOOOON
NNNNN
NNNN

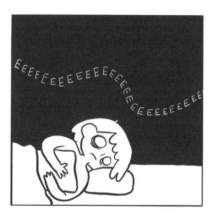

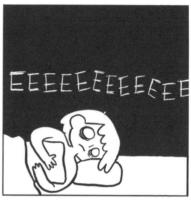

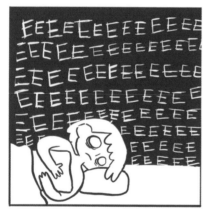

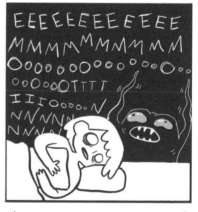

ANXIETY, WHY ARE YOU LIKE THIS?

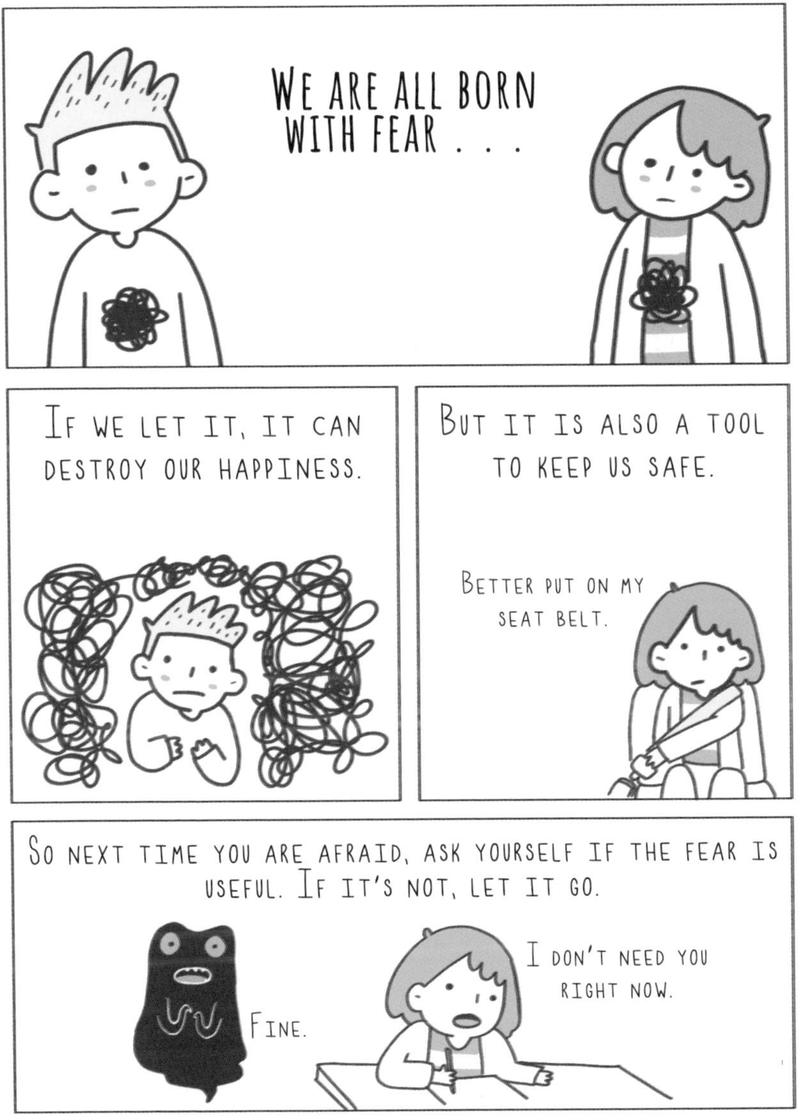
WE ARE ALL BORN WITH FEAR . . .
IF WE LET IT, IT CAN DESTROY OUR HAPPINESS.
BUT IT IS ALSO A TOOL TO KEEP US SAFE.
BETTER PUT ON MY SEAT BELT.
SO NEXT TIME YOU ARE AFRAID, ASK YOURSELF IF THE FEAR IS USEFUL. IF IT'S NOT, LET IT GO.
FINE.
I DON'T NEED YOU RIGHT NOW.

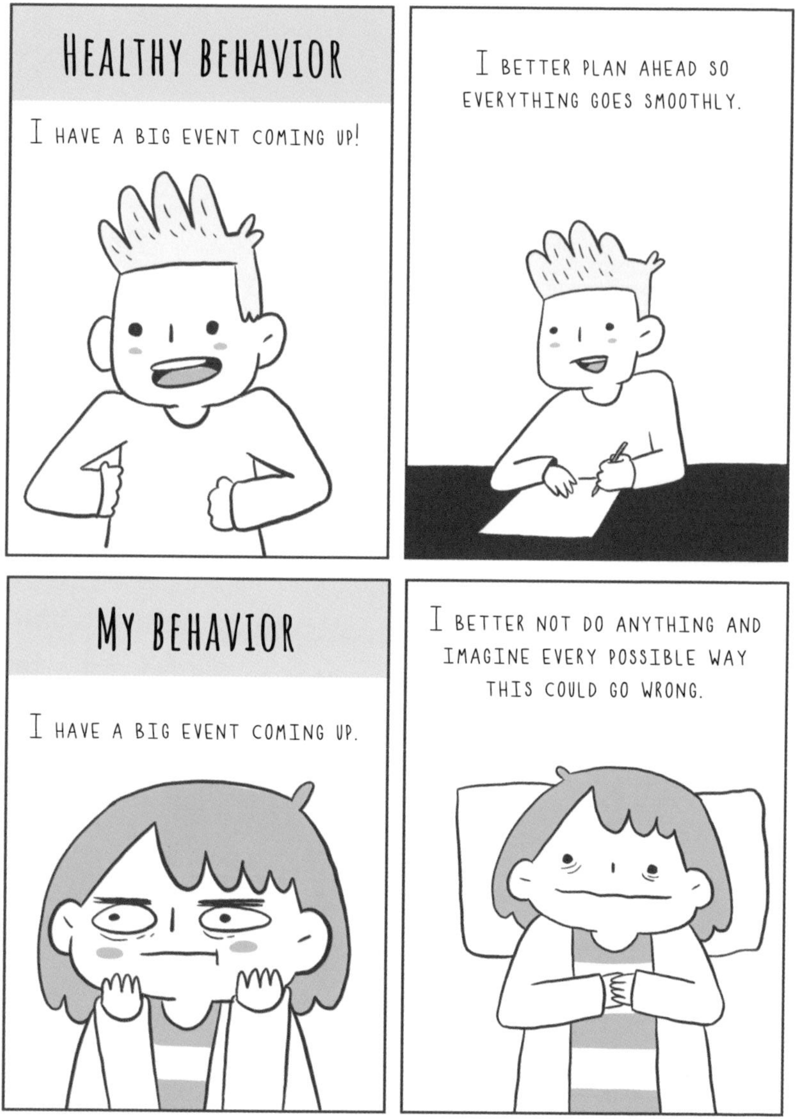
HEALTHY BEHAVIOR
I HAVE A BIG EVENT COMING UP!
I BETTER PLAN AHEAD SO EVERYTHING GOES SMOOTHLY.
MY BEHAVIOR
I HAVE A BIG EVENT COMING UP.
I BETTER NOT DO ANYTHING AND IMAGINE EVERY POSSIBLE WAY THIS COULD GO WRONG.

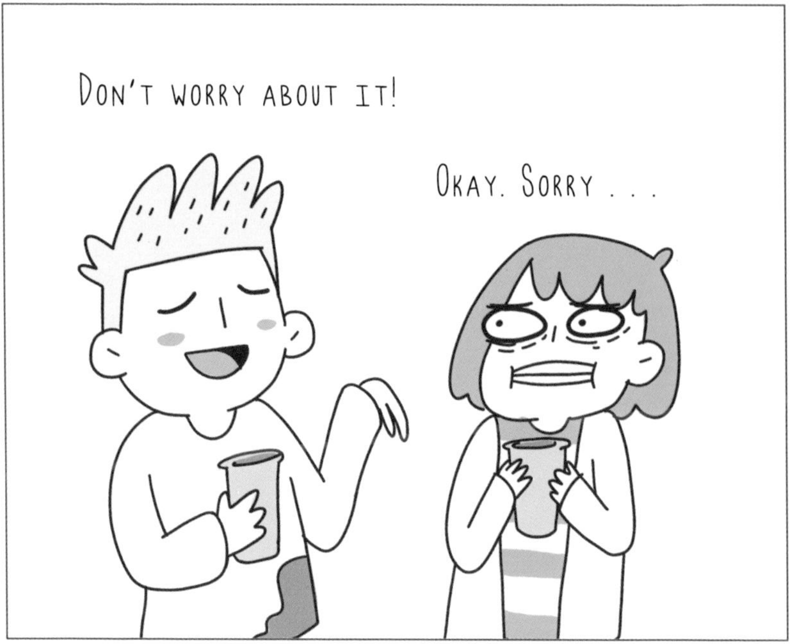
DON'T WORRY ABOUT IT!
OKAY. SORRY . . .

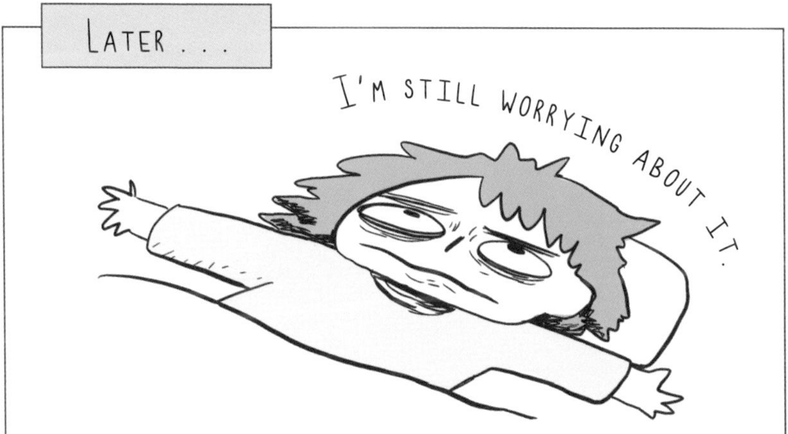
LATER . . .
I'M STILL WORRYING ABOUT IT.

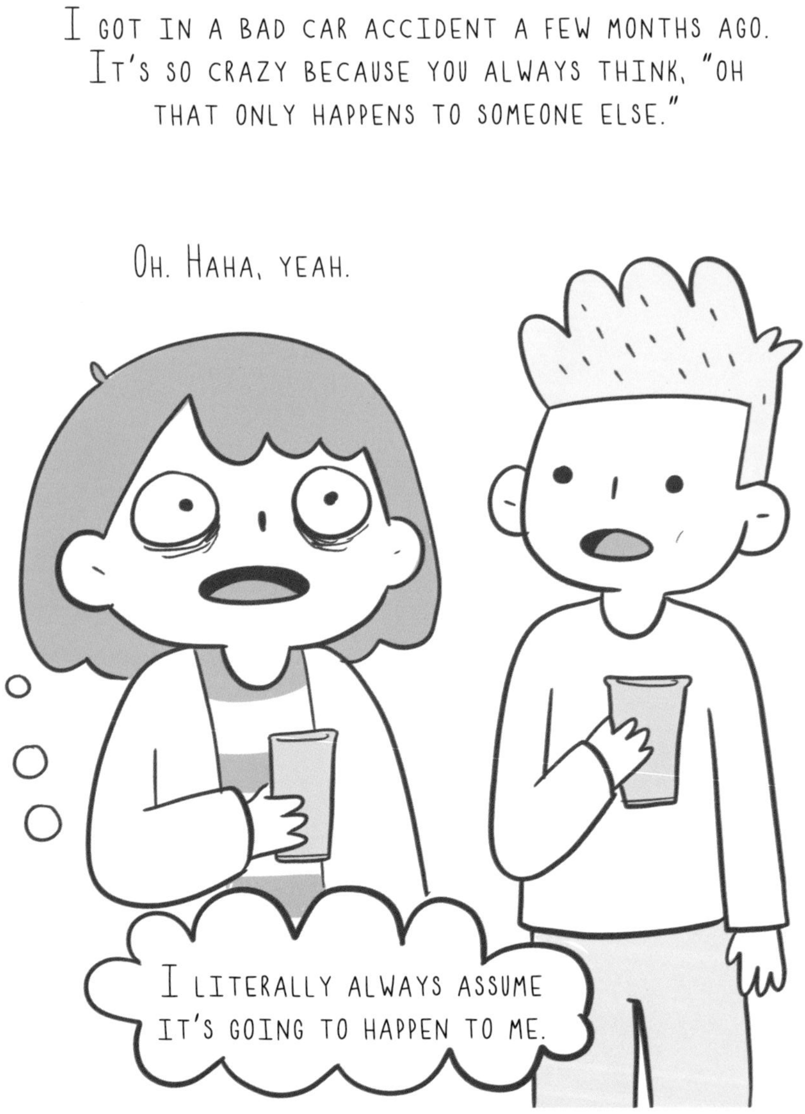
I GOT IN A BAD CAR ACCIDENT A FEW MONTHS AGO. IT'S SO CRAZY BECAUSE YOU ALWAYS THINK, "OH THAT ONLY HAPPENS TO SOMEONE ELSE."
OH. HAHA, YEAH.
I LITERALLY ALWAYS ASSUME IT'S GOING TO HAPPEN TO ME.

I'M STRESSED OUT. WANNA WATCH A DUMB SHOW WITH ME TONIGHT?
SURE!
SCHOOL GOT YOU STRESSED OUT?
NO, IT'S PEOPLE.
IT'S ALWAYS PEOPLE.

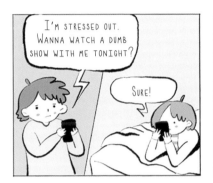

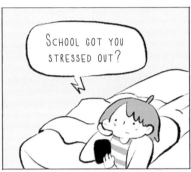

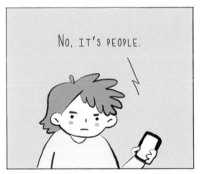

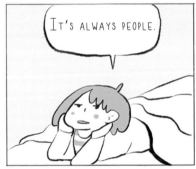

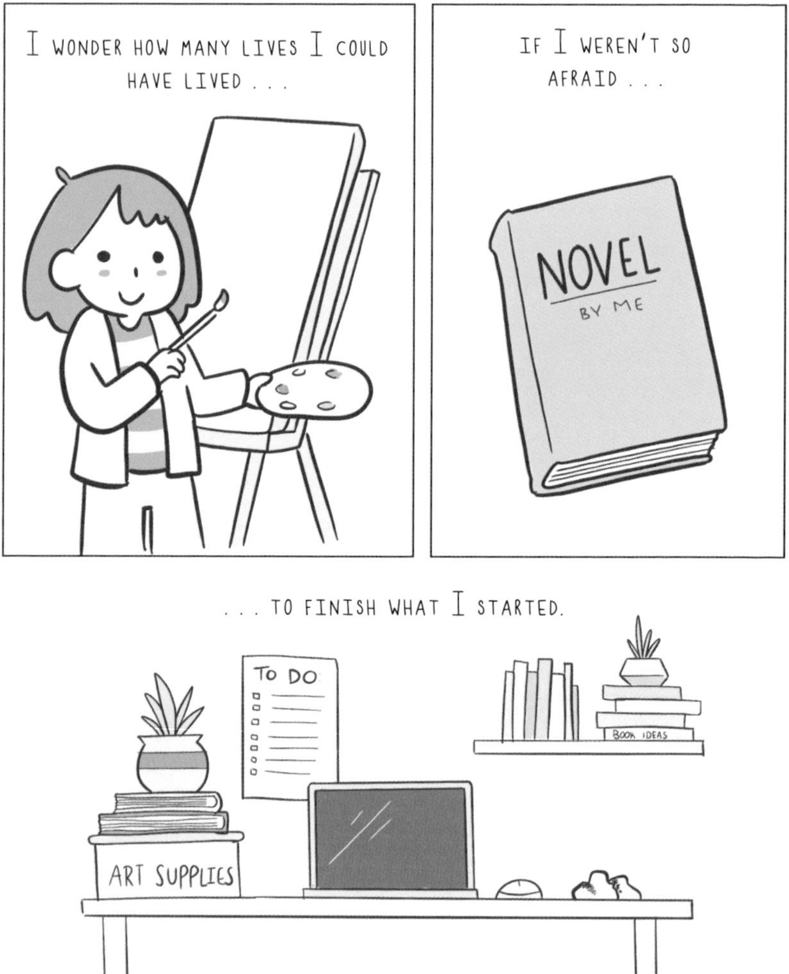
I WONDER HOW MANY LIVES I COULD HAVE LIVED . . .
IF I WEREN'T SO AFRAID . . .
NOVEL
BY ME
. . . TO FINISH WHAT I STARTED.
TO DO
BOOK IDEAS
ART SUPPLIES

HOW ANXIETY MAKES ME FEEL

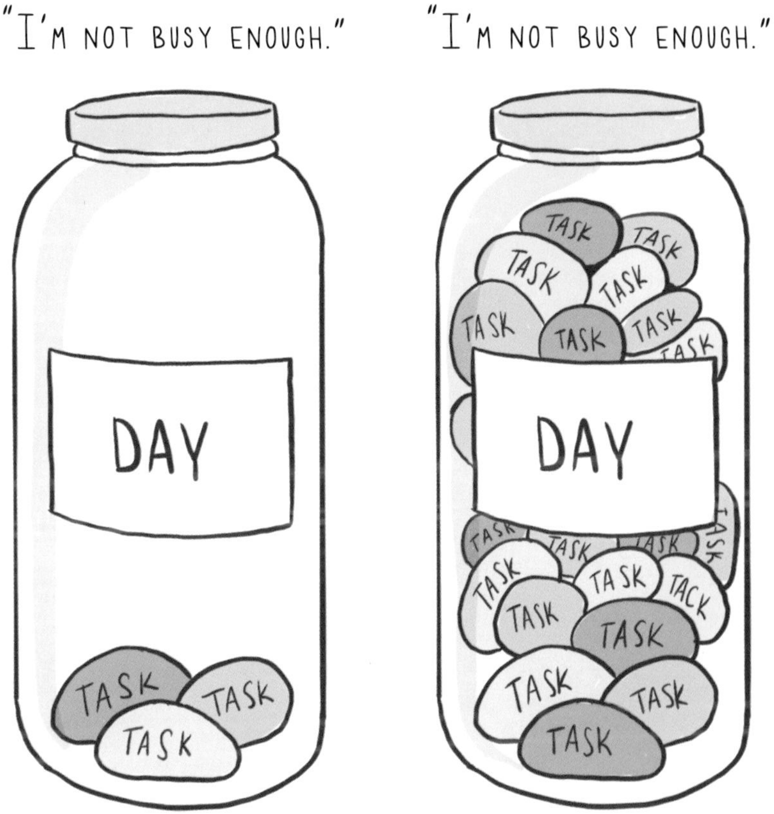
"I'M NOT BUSY ENOUGH."
DAY
TASK
TASK
TASK
"I'M NOT BUSY ENOUGH."
TASK
TASK
TASK
TASK
TASK
TASK
TASK
DAY
TASK
TASK
TASK
TACK
TASK
TASK
TASK
TASK
TASK

A PARADOX:

THINKING A LOT ABOUT TRYING NOT TO THINK TOO MUCH.

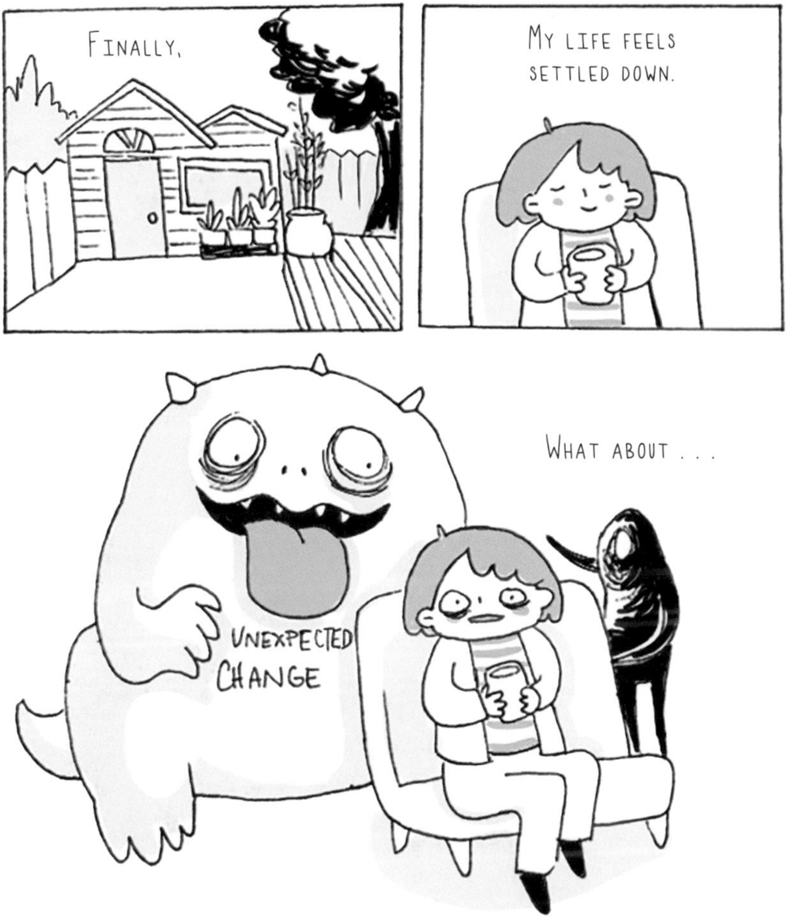
FINALLY,
MY LIFE FEELS SETTLED DOWN.
WHAT ABOUT . . .
UNEXPECTED CHANGE

EVERYTHING'S. FINE.

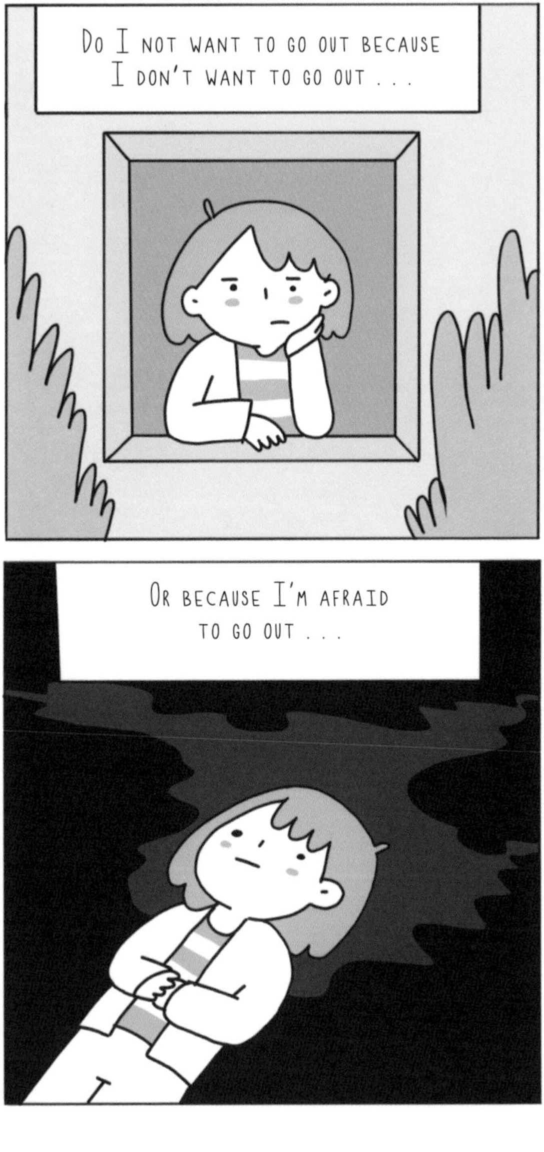
Do I not want to go out because
I don't want to go out . . .
Or because I'm afraid
to go out . . .

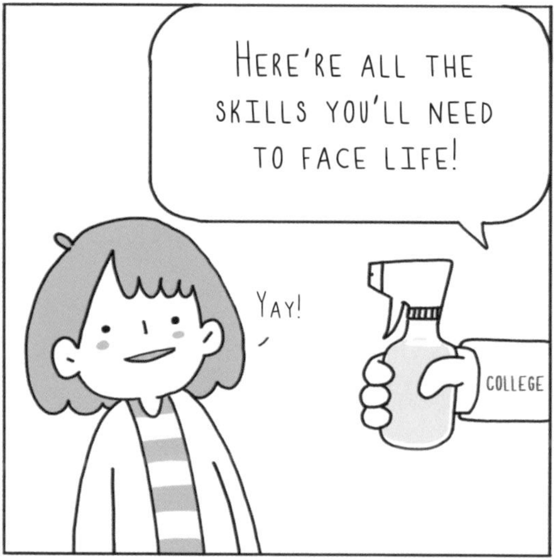
HERE'RE ALL THE SKILLS YOU'LL NEED TO FACE LIFE!
YAY!
COLLEGE

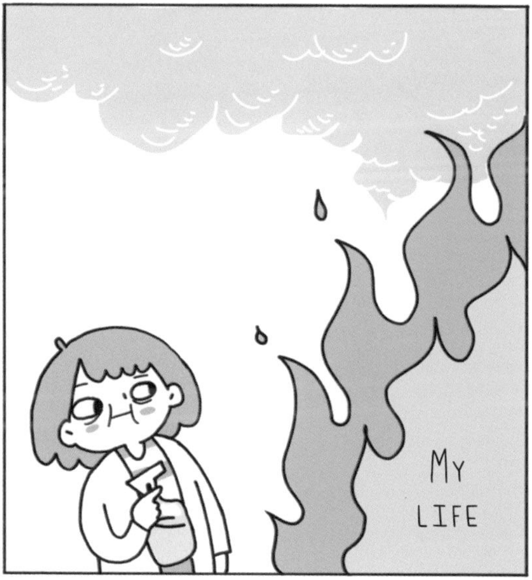
MY LIFE

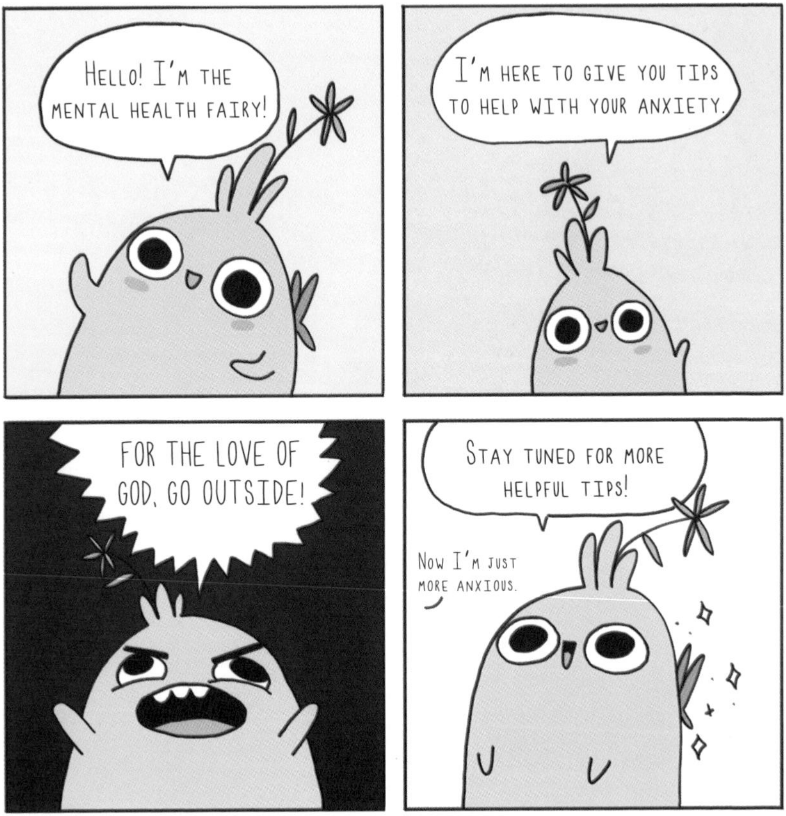
HELLO! I'M THE MENTAL HEALTH FAIRY!
I'M HERE TO GIVE YOU TIPS TO HELP WITH YOUR ANXIETY.
FOR THE LOVE OF GOD, GO OUTSIDE!
STAY TUNED FOR MORE HELPFUL TIPS!
NOW I'M JUST MORE ANXIOUS.

REMEMBER, IT'S OKAY TO MAKE MISTAKES!
MENTAL HEALTH FAIRY
WE ALL MESS UP, LET PEOPLE DOWN, AND HAVE HARD DAYS . . .
. . . EVENTUALLY WE WILL ALL DIE, AND OUR EXISTENCE WILL BE FORGOTTEN FOREVER.
SO, DON'T STRESS THE SMALL STUFF!

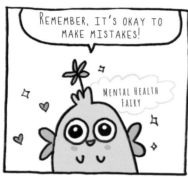

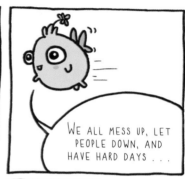

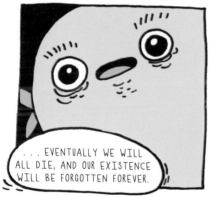

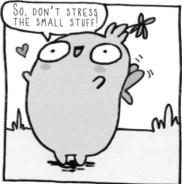

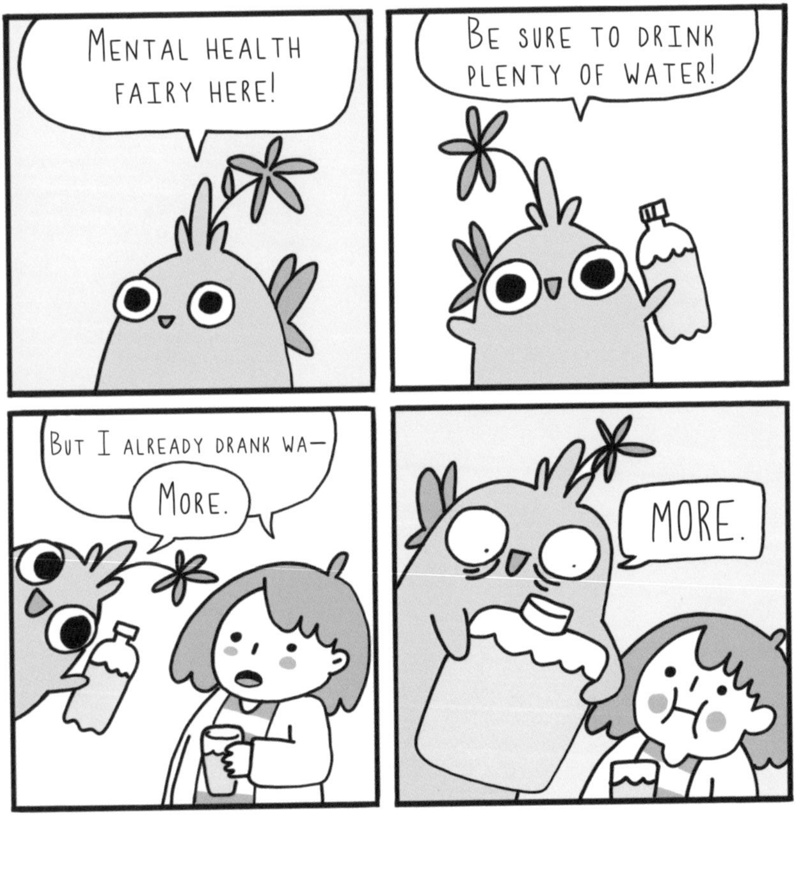
MENTAL HEALTH FAIRY HERE!
BE SURE TO DRINK PLENTY OF WATER!
BUT I ALREADY DRANK WA—
MORE.
MORE.

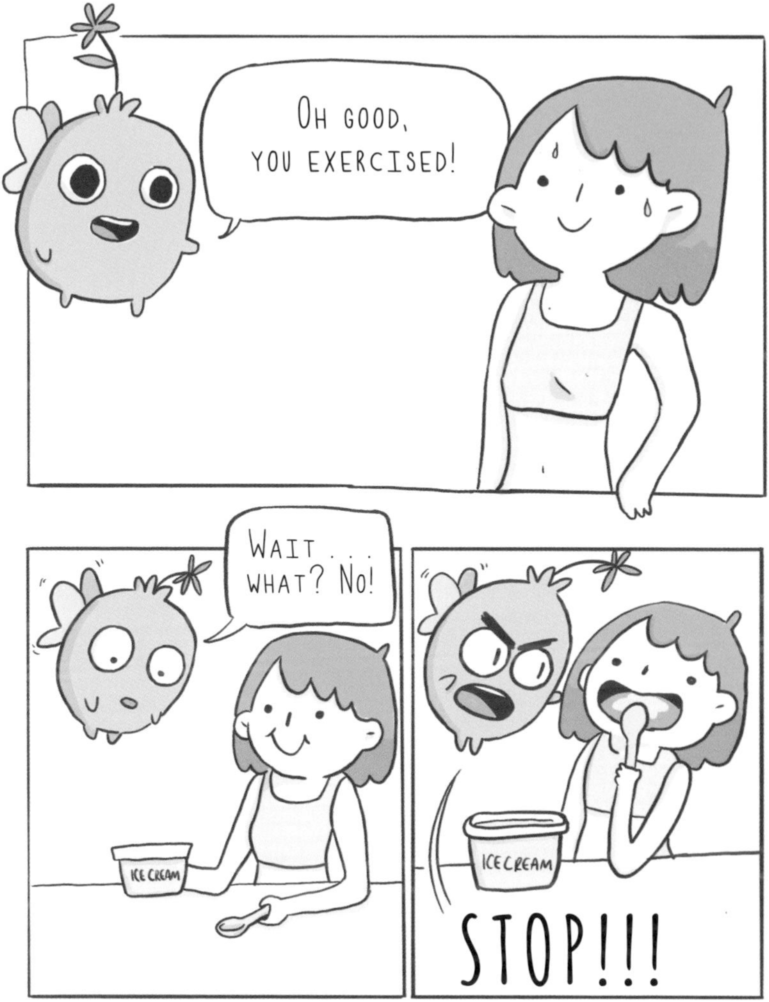
OH GOOD,
YOU EXERCISED!
WAIT . . .
WHAT? NO!
ICE CREAM
ICE CREAM
STOP!!!

ON PANIC ATTACKS:

I USED TO THINK A "PANIC ATTACK" WAS JUST A PHRASE THAT MEANT "FREAKING OUT A LITTLE."

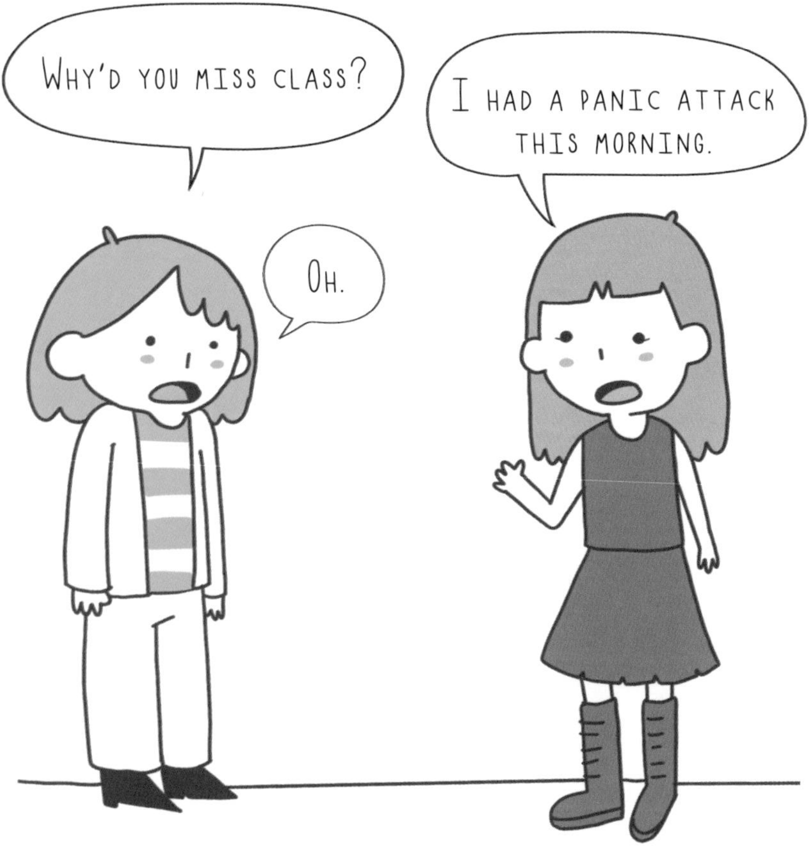
WHY'D YOU MISS CLASS?
I HAD A PANIC ATTACK THIS MORNING.
OH.

MY FRIEND IN COLLEGE USED TO HAVE THEM A LOT, BUT I ALWAYS THOUGHT SHE WAS EXAGGERATING WHEN SHE TALKED ABOUT THEM.

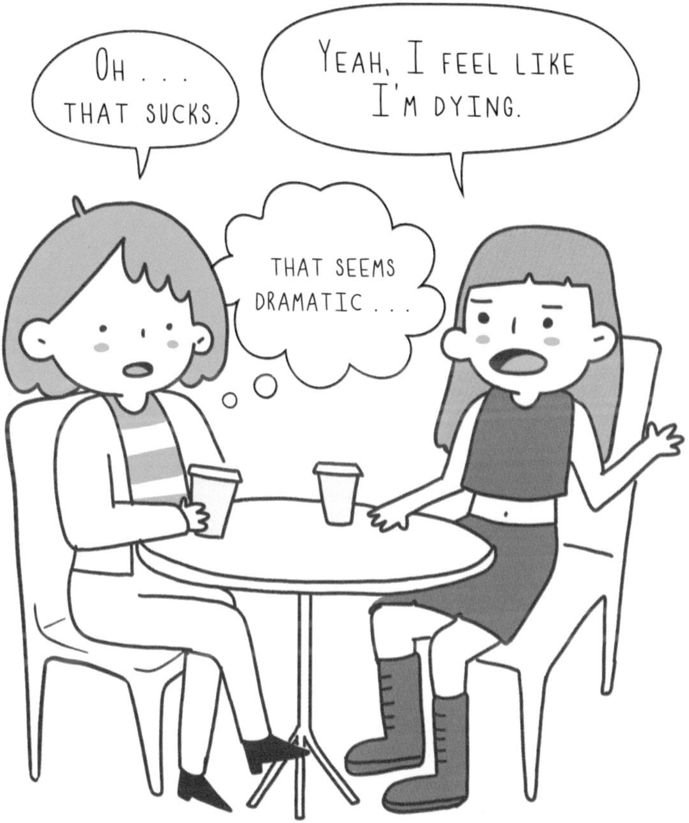
YEAH, I FEEL LIKE I'M DYING.
OH . . . THAT SUCKS.
THAT SEEMS DRAMATIC . . .

BUT THEN I HAD MY FIRST PANIC ATTACK.

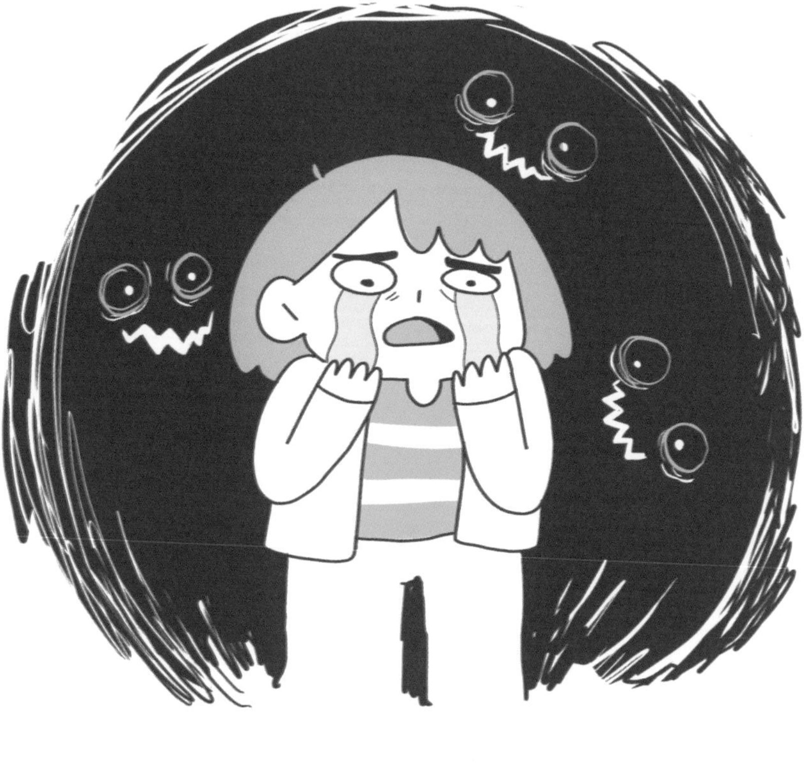

I REALIZED SHE WASN'T EXAGGERATING AT ALL.

I WAS AT A PARTY, AND MY CRUSH WAS PURPOSELY IGNORING ME. I HAD THE OVERWHELMING URGE THAT **I HAD** TO LEAVE OR SOMETHING TERRIBLE WOULD HAPPEN.

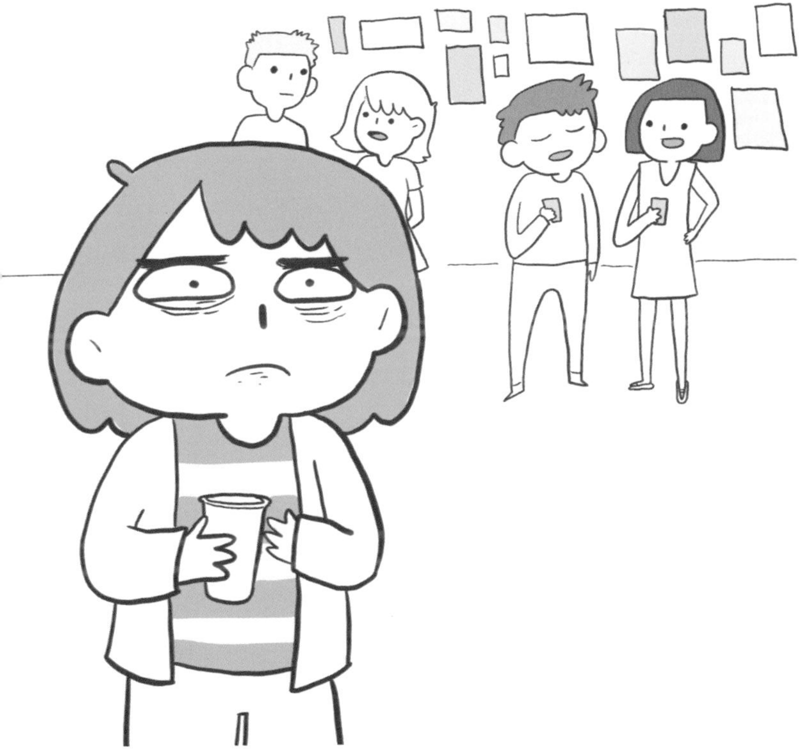

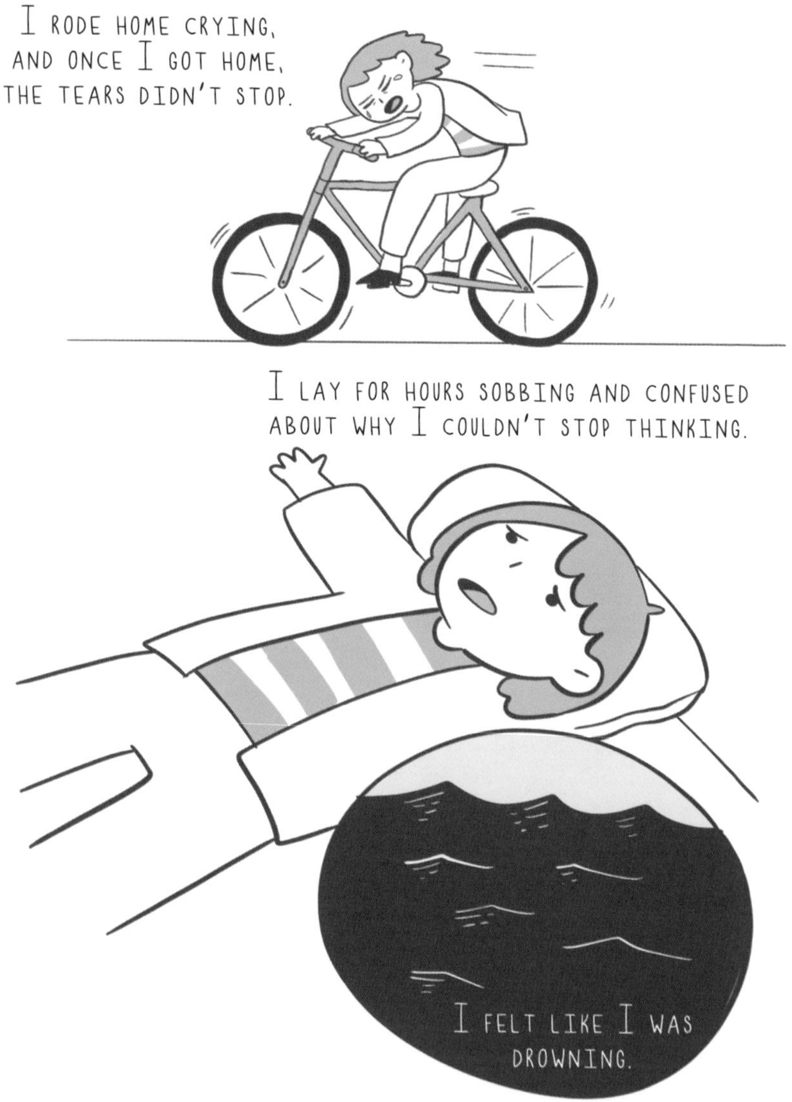
I RODE HOME CRYING, AND ONCE I GOT HOME, THE TEARS DIDN'T STOP.
I LAY FOR HOURS SOBBING AND CONFUSED ABOUT WHY I COULDN'T STOP THINKING.
I FELT LIKE I WAS DROWNING.

My thoughts were on loop

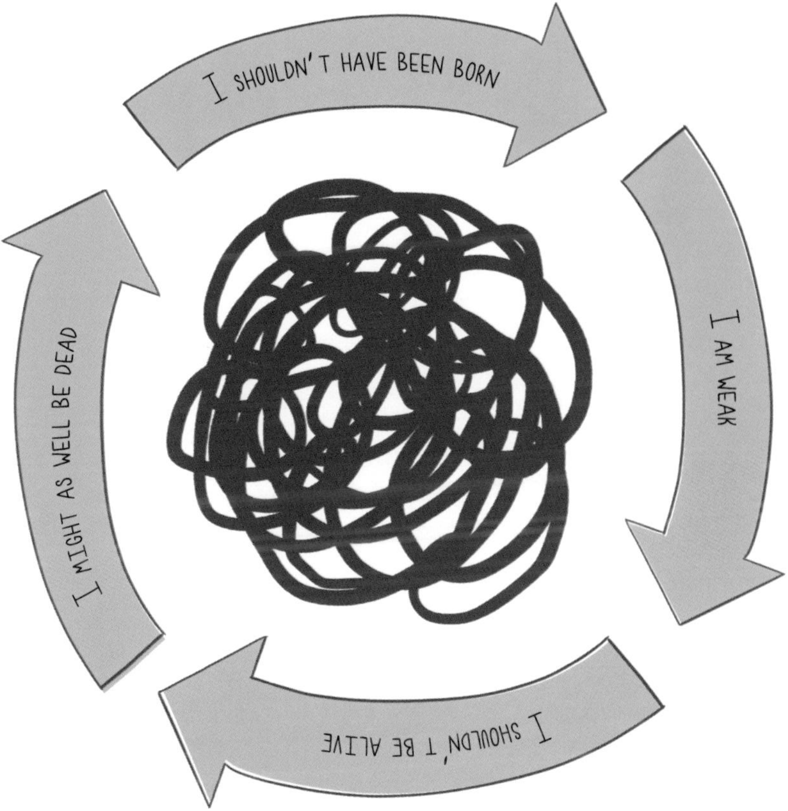
I shouldn't have been born
I am weak
I shouldn't be alive
I might as well be dead

It took me a few days to realize it was a panic attack.

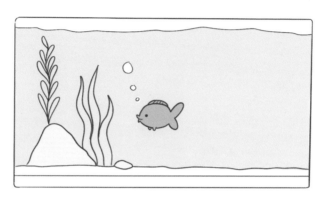

I described what happened to my dad, and he said, "Oh yeah, that's a panic attack. I used to have them multiple times a day in college. I also had agoraphobia for a few years."

He had never told me before. I wish he had.

MY PANIC ATTACK TAUGHT ME THAT MY EMOTIONS
AREN'T ALWAYS IN MY CONTROL AND THAT MENTAL
HEALTH IS ACTUALLY PART OF PHYSICAL HEALTH.

I MEAN, IT MAKES SENSE.

AFTER ALL, MY SAD ASSHOLE BRAIN IS PARTIALLY
IN CHARGE OF MY BODY AND MY THOUGHTS.

Now I have learned some tricks to help my brain calm down during a panic attack.

Meditation

Meditating is like magic. I don't know how it works, but usually after I meditate for even a few minutes, I feel calm for a few hours afterward.

Deep breathing

If I feel like I am having a panic attack, I take notice of my breath. I breathe in for 8 seconds and exhale for 12 seconds. Breathing into a pillow helps, too.

Phone a friend

Talking with someone is often the last thing I want to do during a panic attack, but I force myself to do it. Talking shit about Anime with little brothers is particularly effective.

Decatastrophize

Realizing that I probably won't even remember why I was freaking out in a few months puts it in perspective. A lot of mountains really are just adorable molehills.

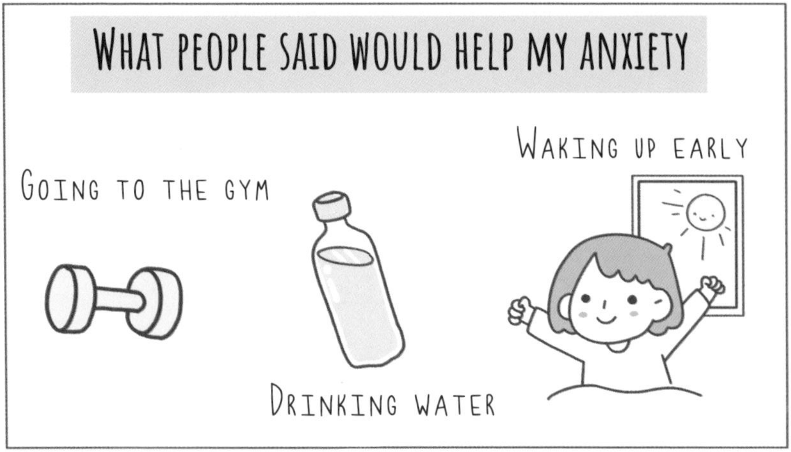
WHAT PEOPLE SAID WOULD HELP MY ANXIETY
GOING TO THE GYM
DRINKING WATER
WAKING UP EARLY

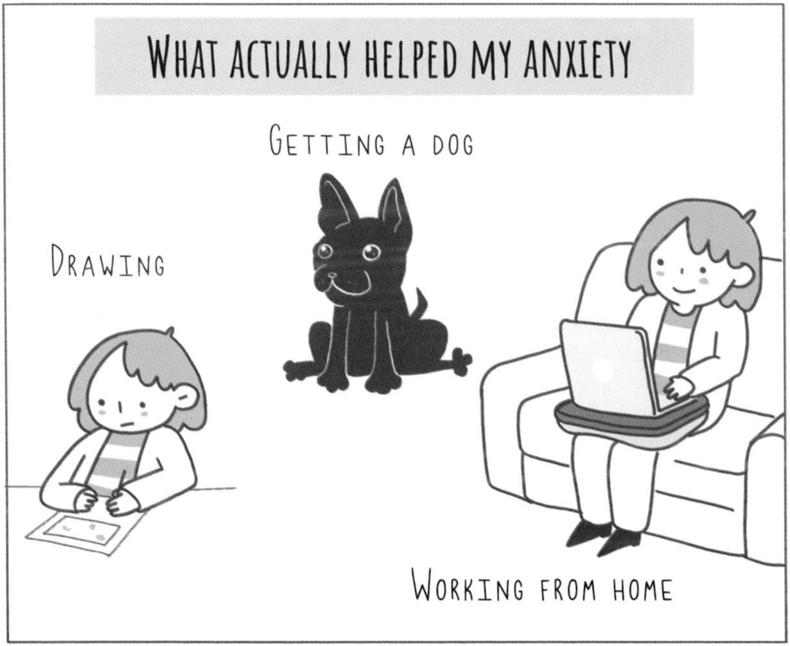
WHAT ACTUALLY HELPED MY ANXIETY
DRAWING
GETTING A DOG
WORKING FROM HOME

SOMETIMES I REACH A POINT OF STRESS AND ANXIETY WHERE I JUST SAY:

SCREW IT!

I'M GOING TO CUT MYSELF SOME SLACK AND JUST DO NOTHING FOR A BIT.

UNSURPRISINGLY, NOTHING TERRIBLE HAPPENS IF I TAKE A BREAK.

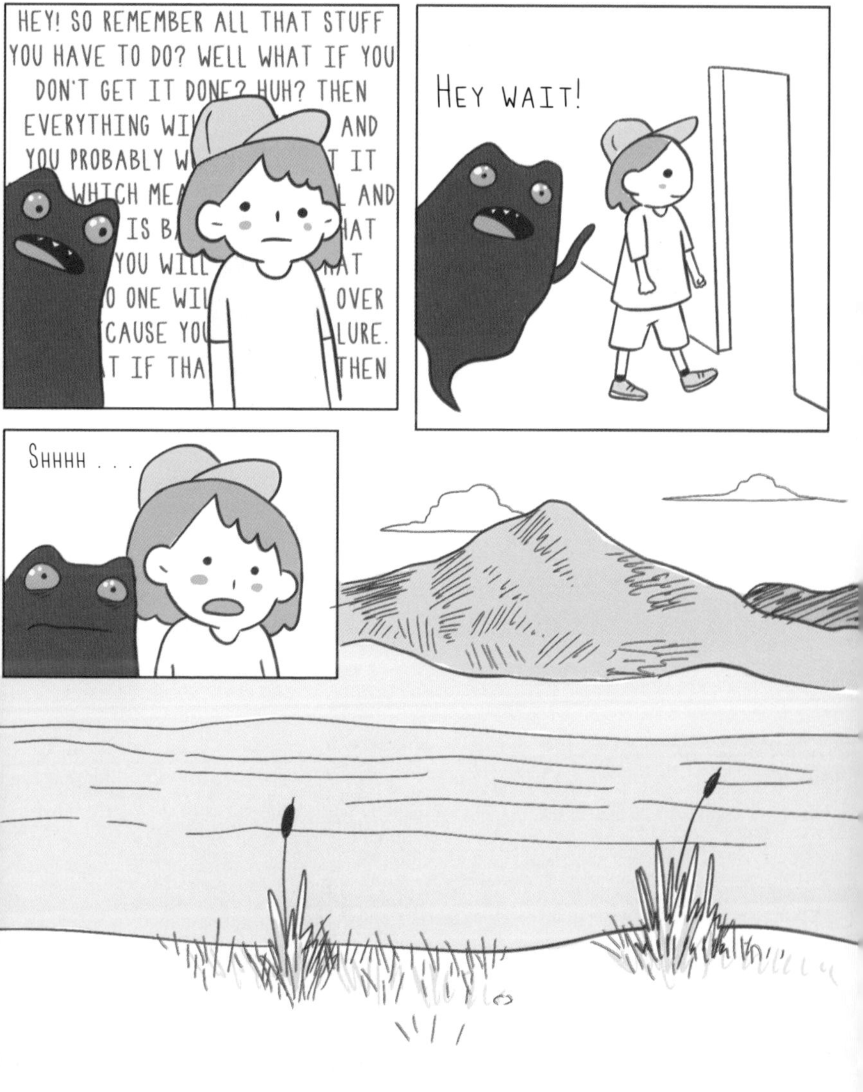

HEY! SO REMEMBER ALL THAT STUFF
YOU HAVE TO DO? WELL WHAT IF YOU
DON'T GET IT DON
HUH? THEN
EVERYTHING WI
AND
YOU PROBABLY W
T IT
WHICH ME
L AND
IS B
HAT
YOU WILL
HAT
O ONE WI
OVER
CAUSE YO
LURE.
T IF THA
THEN
HEY WAIT!
SHHHH . . .
IT CAN WAIT.

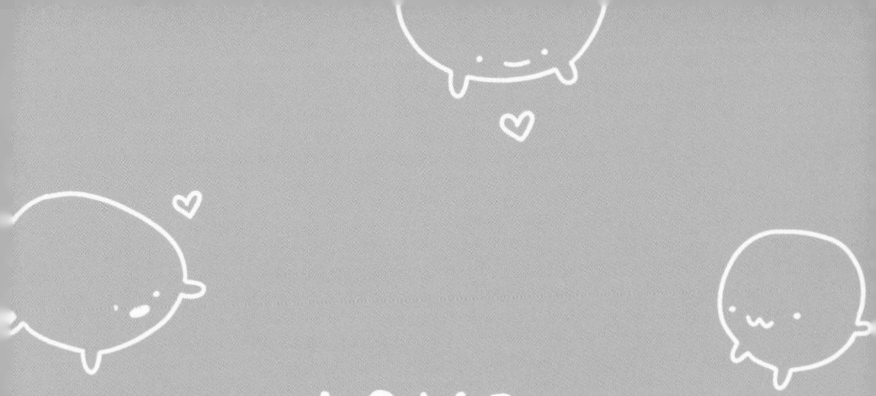

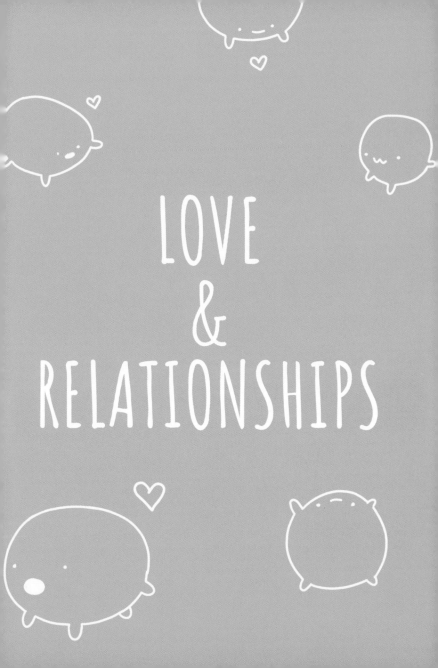

LOVE & RELATIONSHIPS

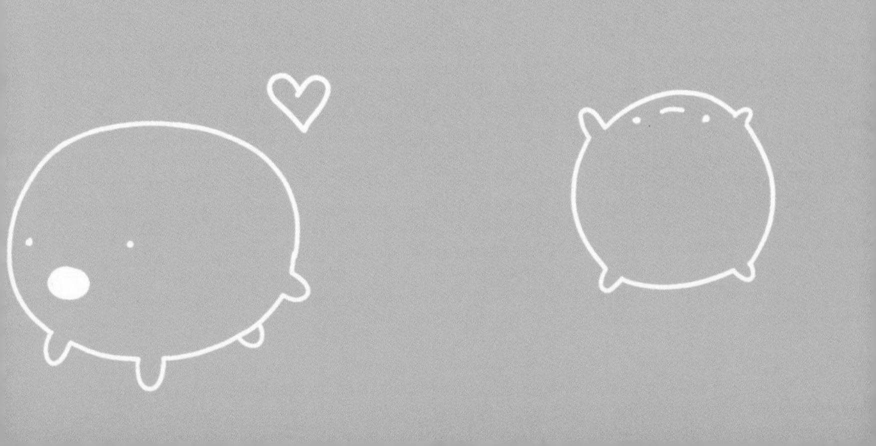

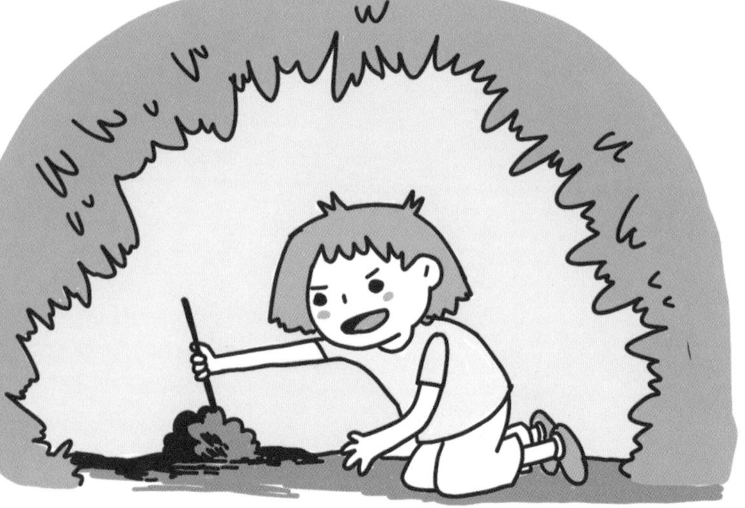

I HOPE EVERY DAY THAT I WILL MAKE MY NINE-YEAR-OLD SELF PROUD.

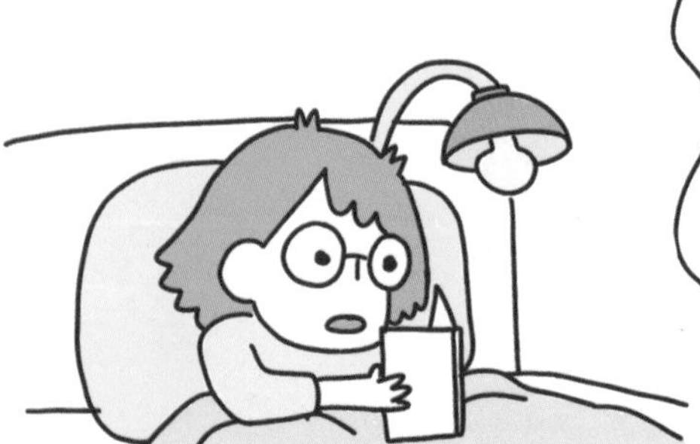

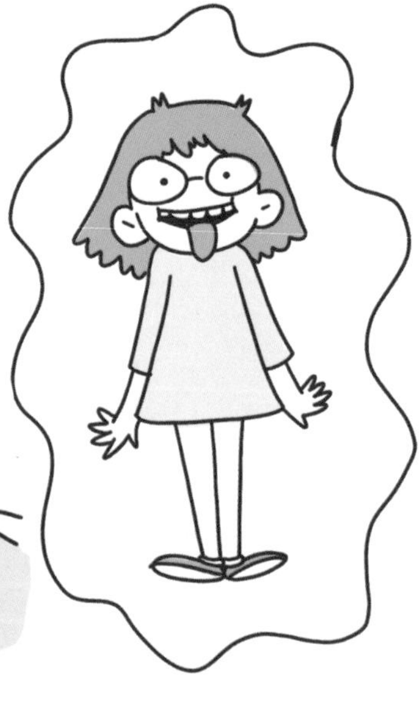

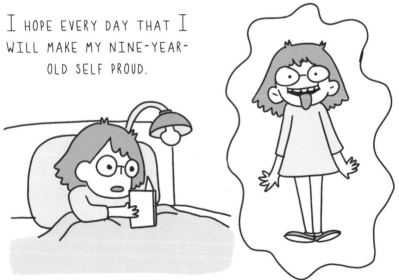

I missed the class where they teach middle-school girls handwriting.

INSTEAD, I WRITE WITH SERIAL KILLER HANDWRITING.

THE THREE BOYFRIENDS

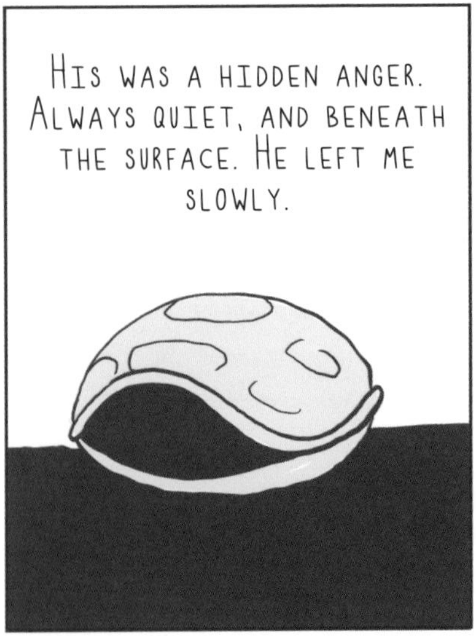
HIS WAS A HIDDEN ANGER. ALWAYS QUIET, AND BENEATH THE SURFACE. HE LEFT ME SLOWLY.

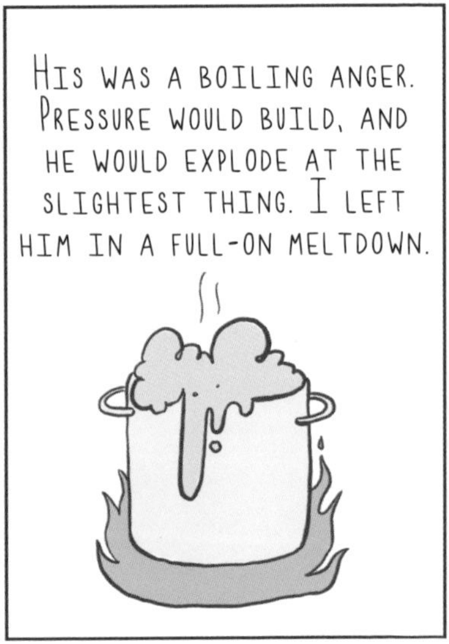
HIS WAS A BOILING ANGER. PRESSURE WOULD BUILD, AND HE WOULD EXPLODE AT THE SLIGHTEST THING. I LEFT HIM IN A FULL-ON MELTDOWN.

HIS WAS AN ANGER I COULD UNDERSTAND. IT WAS QUICK LIKE LIGHTNING. OVER IN A FLASH. FROM THE DESTRUCTION, NEW GROWTH SOMETIMES AROSE.

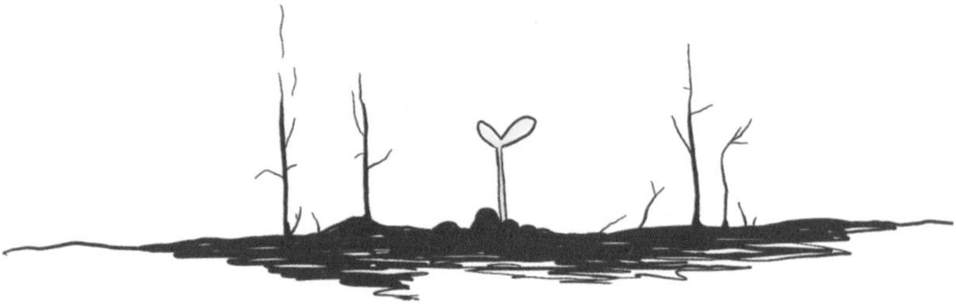

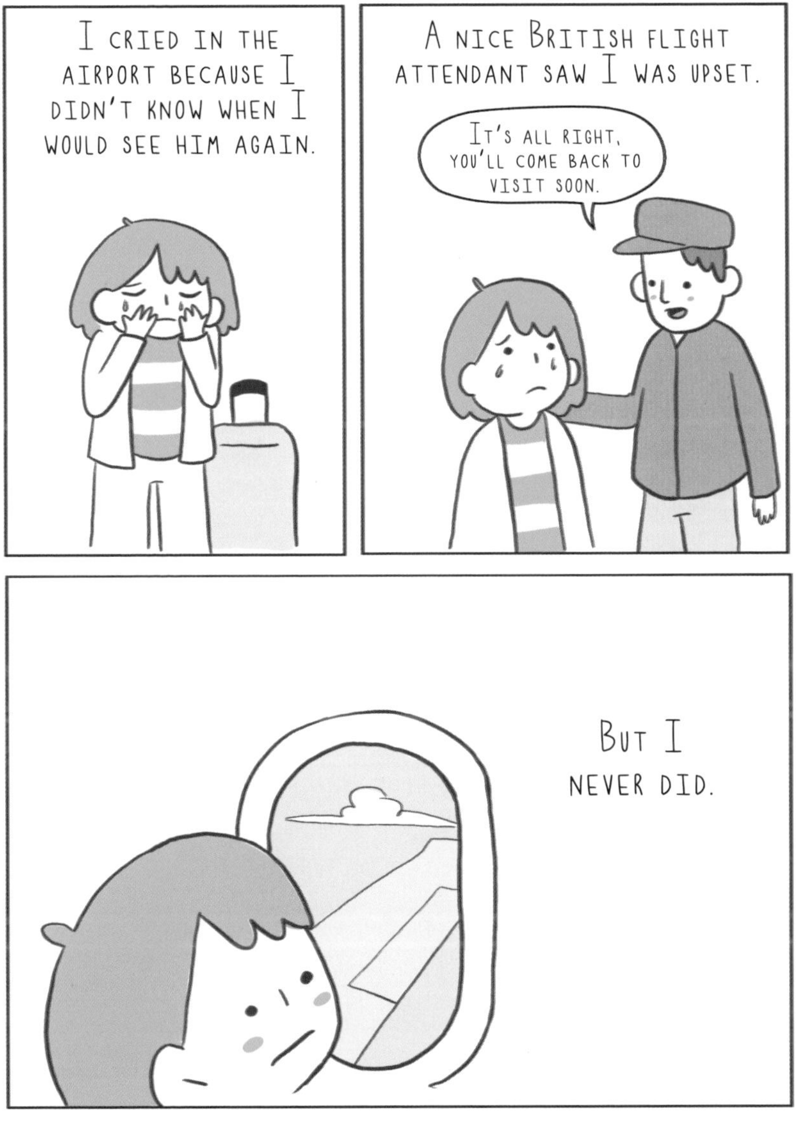
I CRIED IN THE AIRPORT BECAUSE I DIDN'T KNOW WHEN I WOULD SEE HIM AGAIN.
A NICE BRITISH FLIGHT ATTENDANT SAW I WAS UPSET.
IT'S ALL RIGHT, YOU'LL COME BACK TO VISIT SOON.
BUT I NEVER DID.

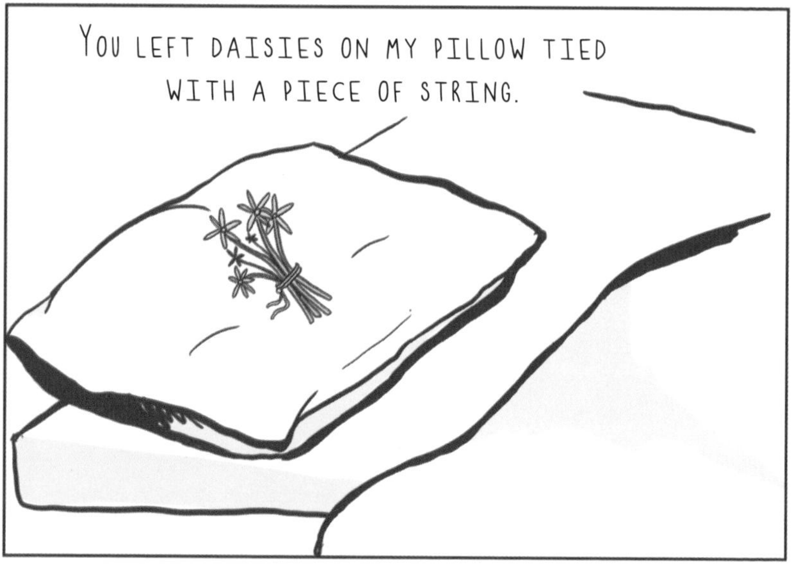
YOU LEFT DAISIES ON MY PILLOW TIED
WITH A PIECE OF STRING.

RAIN PATTERED ON THE
TIN ROOF THAT MORNING.

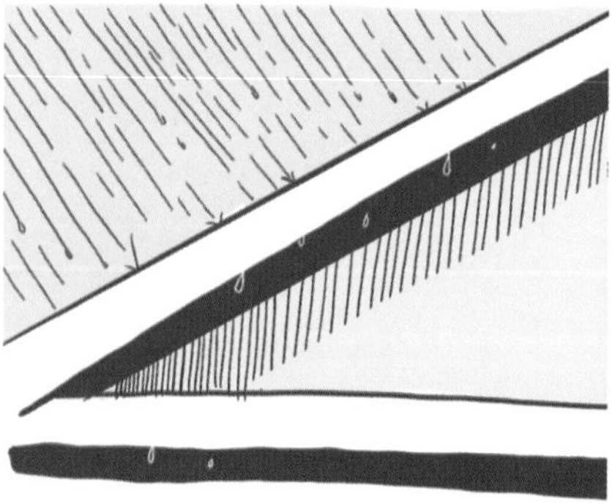

THEN, LIKE THE SUMMER
SUNFLOWERS, YOU WERE GONE.

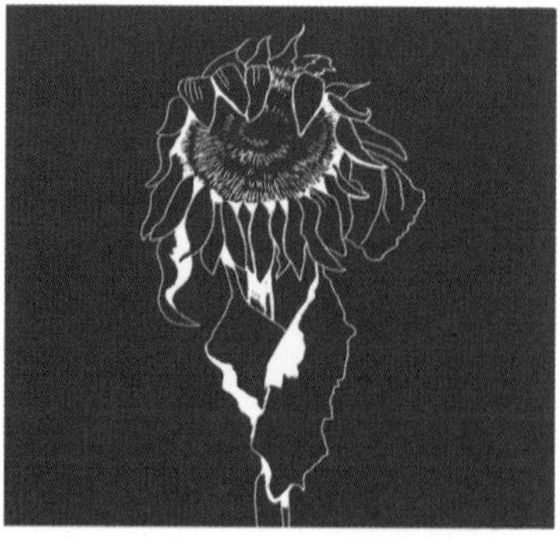

My relationship of two years ended over a chicken sandwich.

He started screaming at me while driving 95 MPH down the highway because I wouldn't give him the first bite of mine.

I told him, "I don't feel safe." And he said, "I don't care."

I broke up with him the next day.
And damn if it wasn't a good sandwich.

FOR A LONG TIME, I THOUGHT I HAD FOUND MYSELF . . .

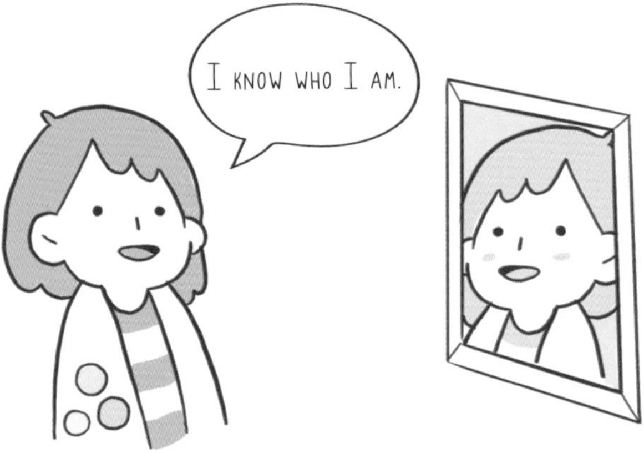
I KNOW WHO I AM.

. . . BUT THEN I LOOKED AROUND AND REALIZED I HAD TRIED TO BECOME WHO OTHERS WANTED ME TO BE.

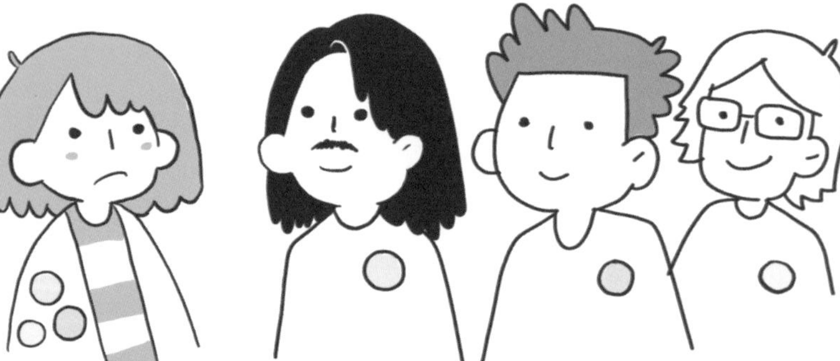

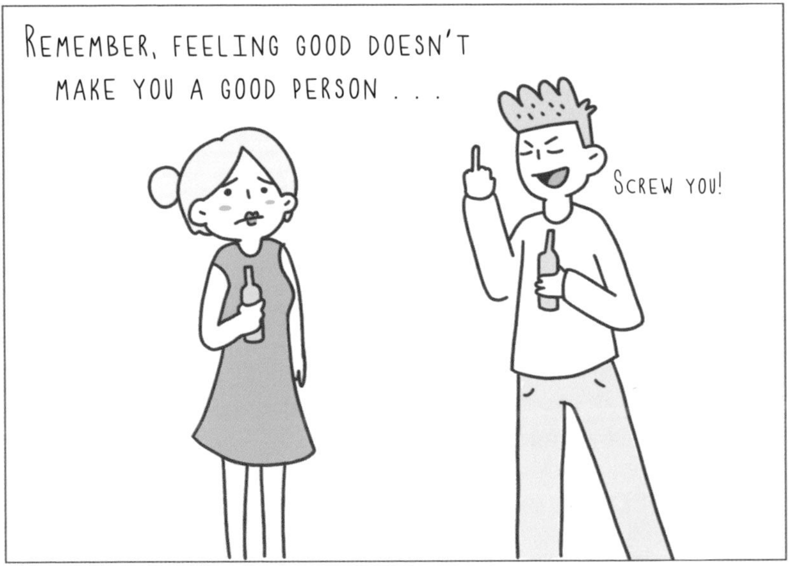
REMEMBER, FEELING GOOD DOESN'T MAKE YOU A GOOD PERSON . . .
SCREW YOU!

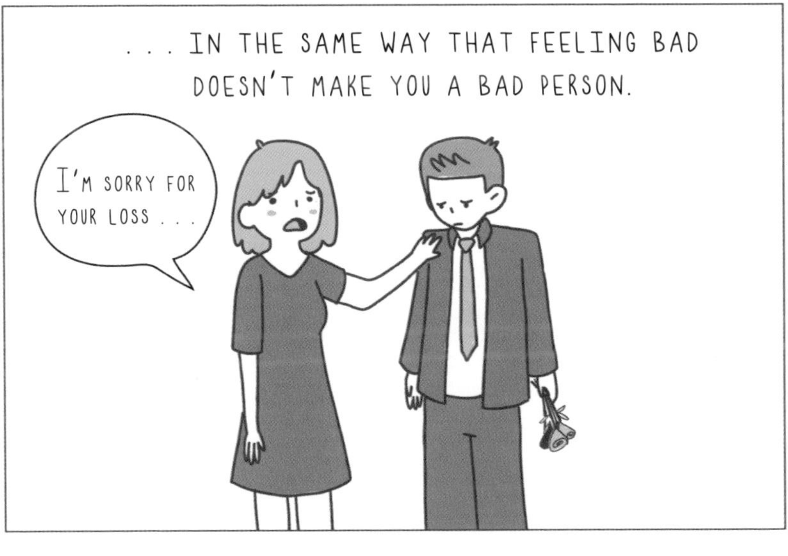
. . . IN THE SAME WAY THAT FEELING BAD DOESN'T MAKE YOU A BAD PERSON.
I'M SORRY FOR YOUR LOSS . . .

OF ALL THE INJUSTICES WOMEN FACE IN LIFE, SMALL POCKETS ARE BY FAR THE MOST INSIDIOUS BECAUSE IT FEELS SO SILLY TO COMPLAIN ABOUT THEM.

My dad's thoughts about tattoos

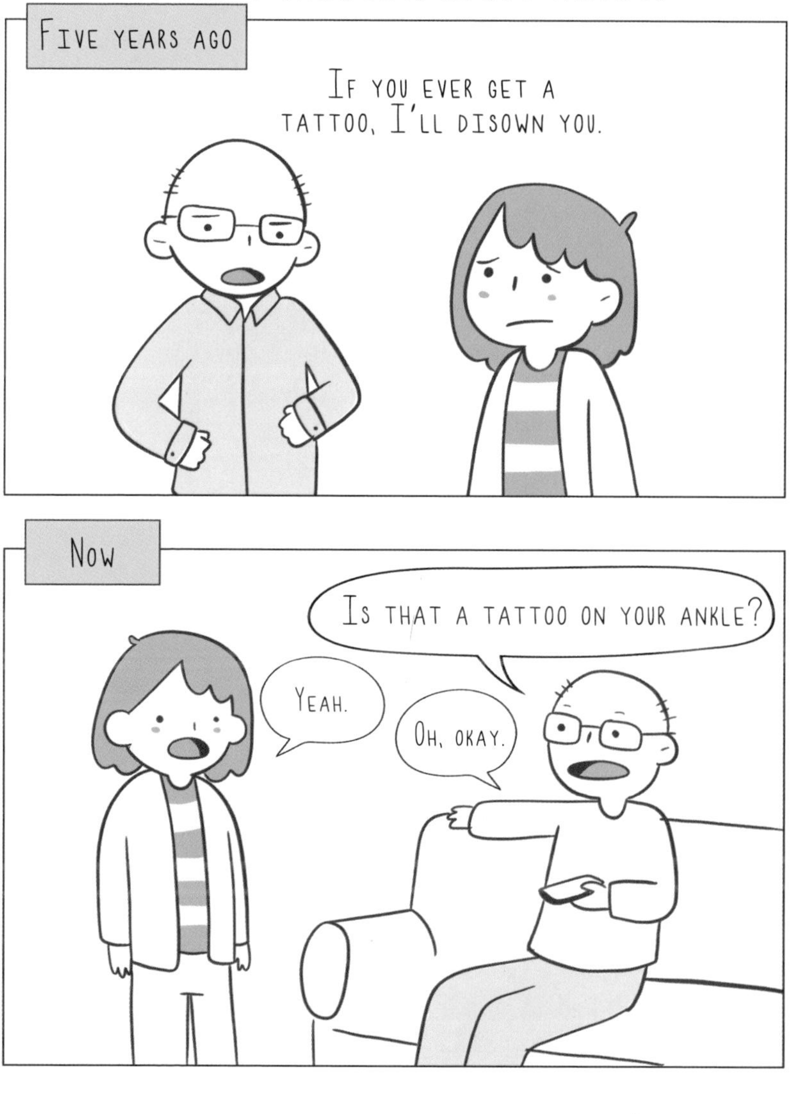
Five years ago
If you ever get a tattoo, I'll disown you.
Now
Is that a tattoo on your ankle?
Yeah.
Oh, okay.

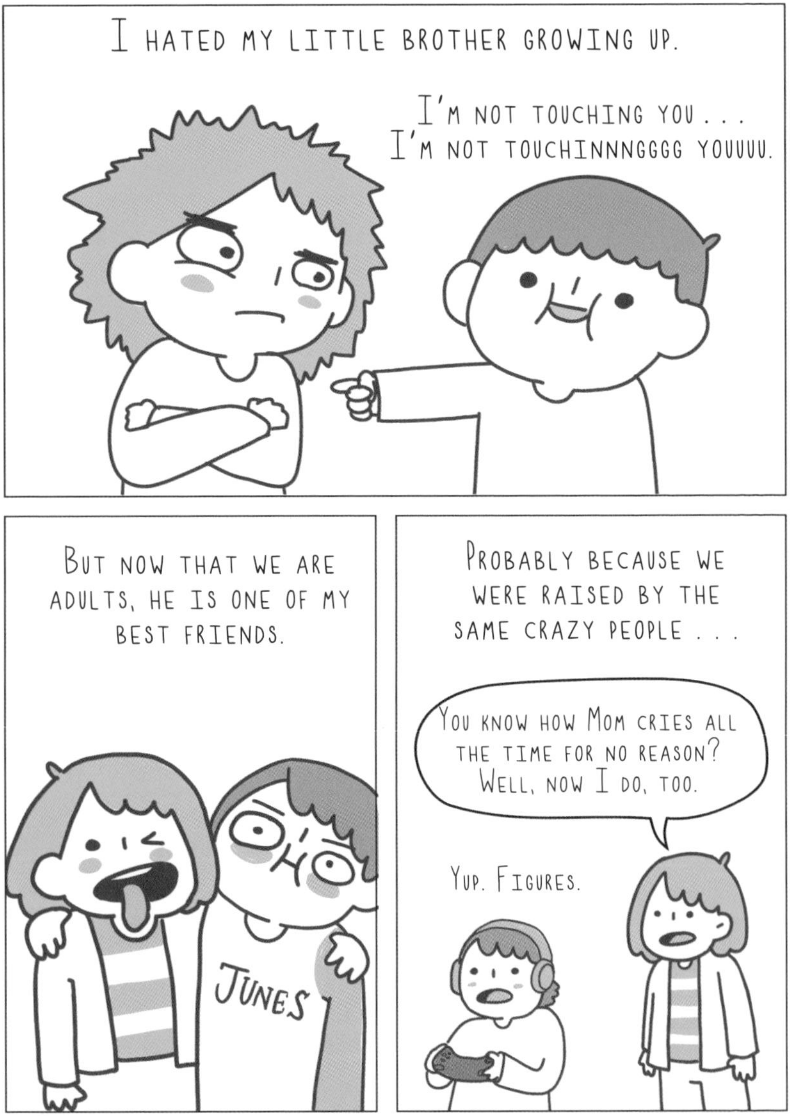
I HATED MY LITTLE BROTHER GROWING UP.
I'M NOT TOUCHING YOU . . .
I'M NOT TOUCHINNNGGGG YOUUUU.
BUT NOW THAT WE ARE ADULTS, HE IS ONE OF MY BEST FRIENDS.
JUNES
PROBABLY BECAUSE WE WERE RAISED BY THE SAME CRAZY PEOPLE . . .
YOU KNOW HOW MOM CRIES ALL THE TIME FOR NO REASON? WELL, NOW I DO, TOO.
YUP. FIGURES.

DIVORCE:

Two houses

Two phone calls

Hey dad.

Hey mom.

Too many things that can't be fixed.

Perks of seeing old friends

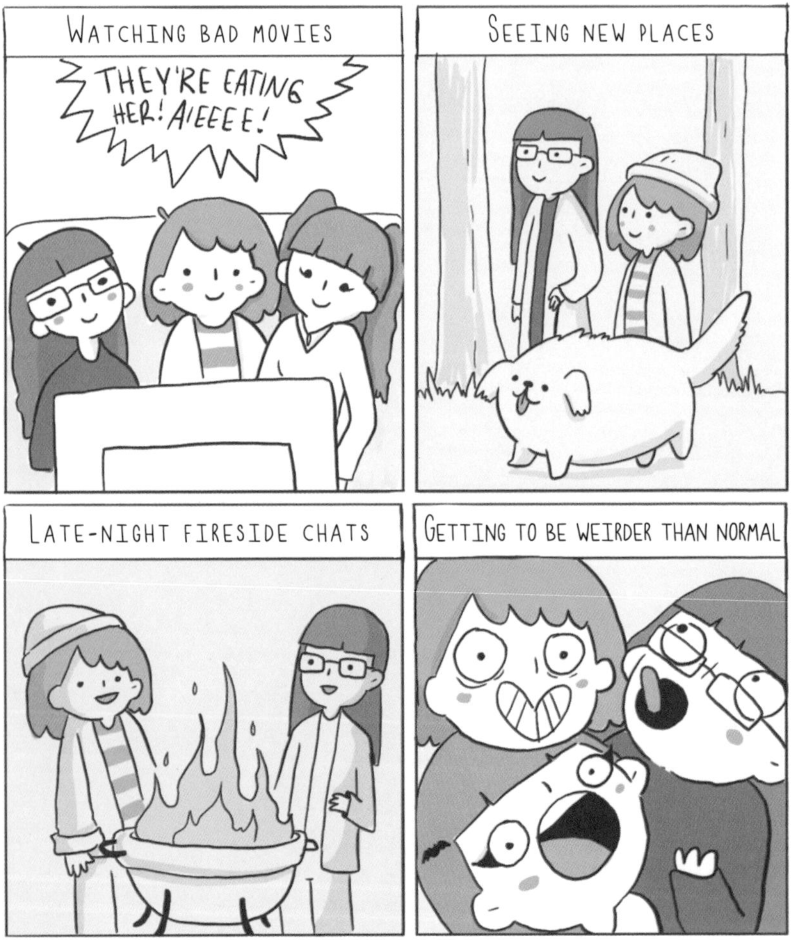
Watching bad movies
THEY'RE EATING HER! AIEEEE!
Seeing new places
Late-night fireside chats
Getting to be weirder than normal

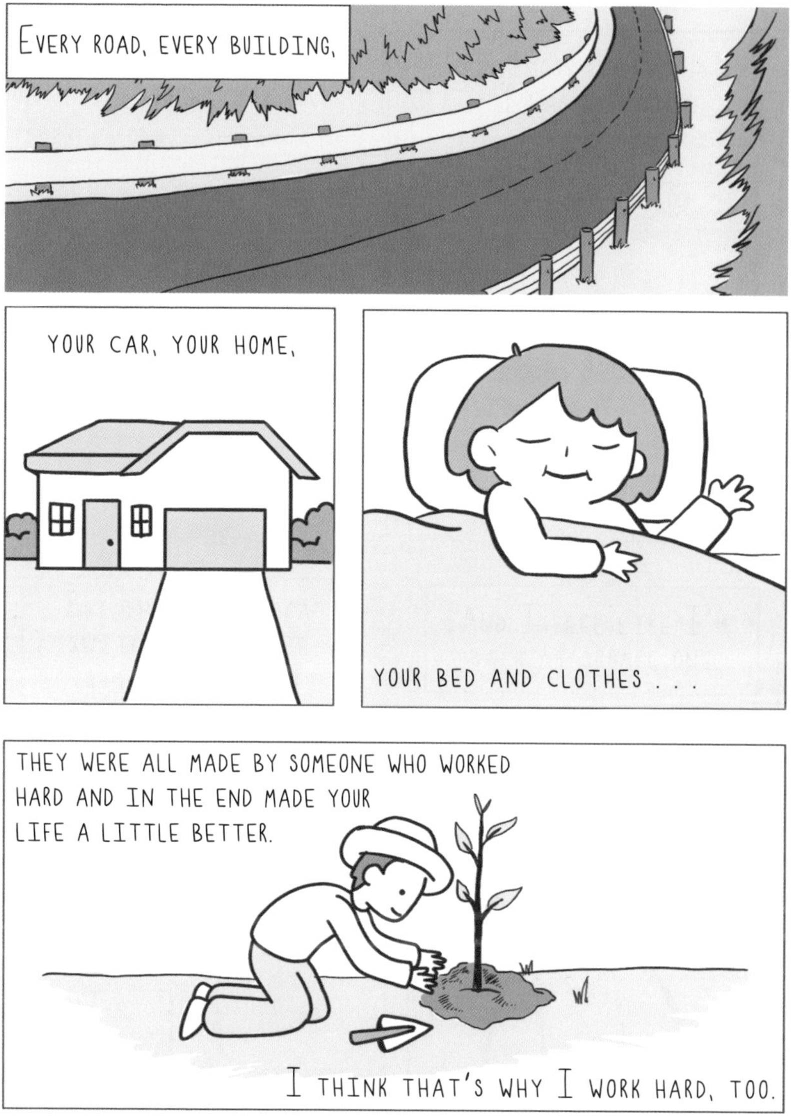
EVERY ROAD, EVERY BUILDING,
YOUR CAR, YOUR HOME,
YOUR BED AND CLOTHES . . .
THEY WERE ALL MADE BY SOMEONE WHO WORKED HARD AND IN THE END MADE YOUR LIFE A LITTLE BETTER.
I THINK THAT'S WHY I WORK HARD, TOO.

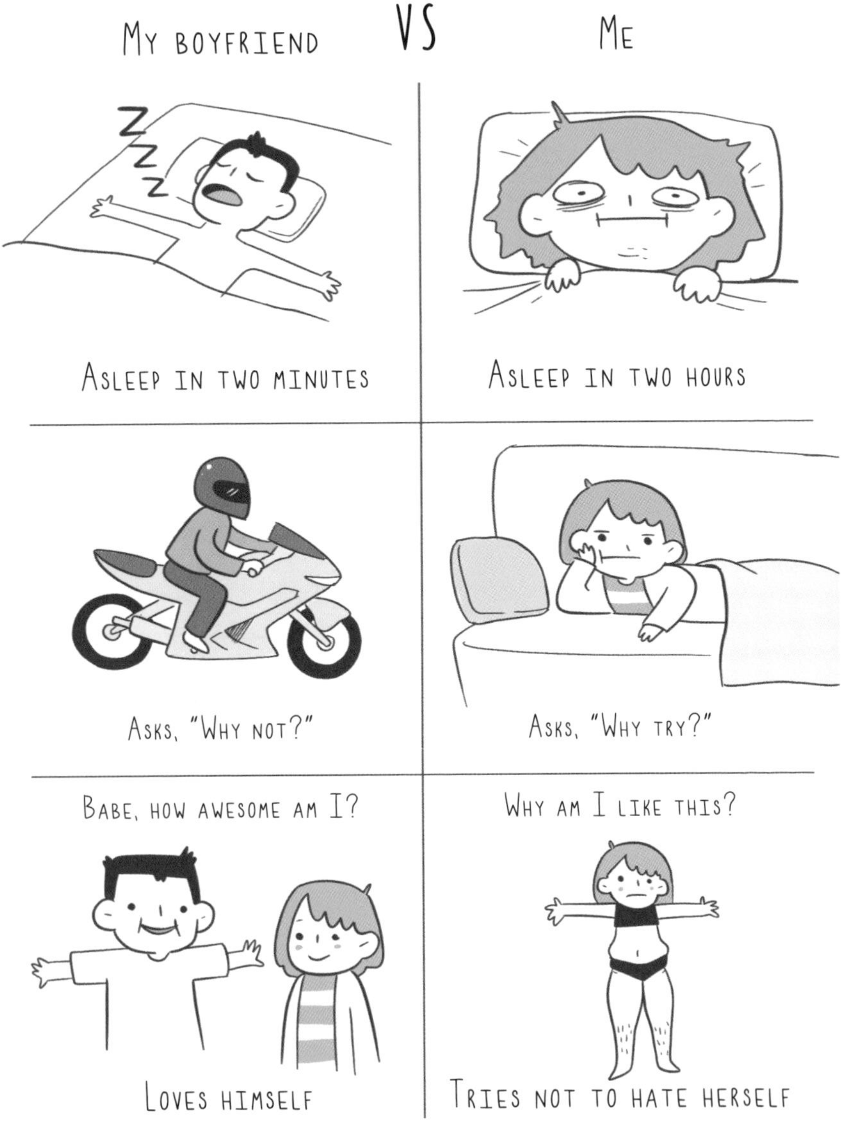
MY BOYFRIEND
VS
ME
ASLEEP IN TWO MINUTES
ASLEEP IN TWO HOURS
ASKS, "WHY NOT?"
ASKS, "WHY TRY?"
BABE, HOW AWESOME AM I?
LOVES HIMSELF
WHY AM I LIKE THIS?
TRIES NOT TO HATE HERSELF

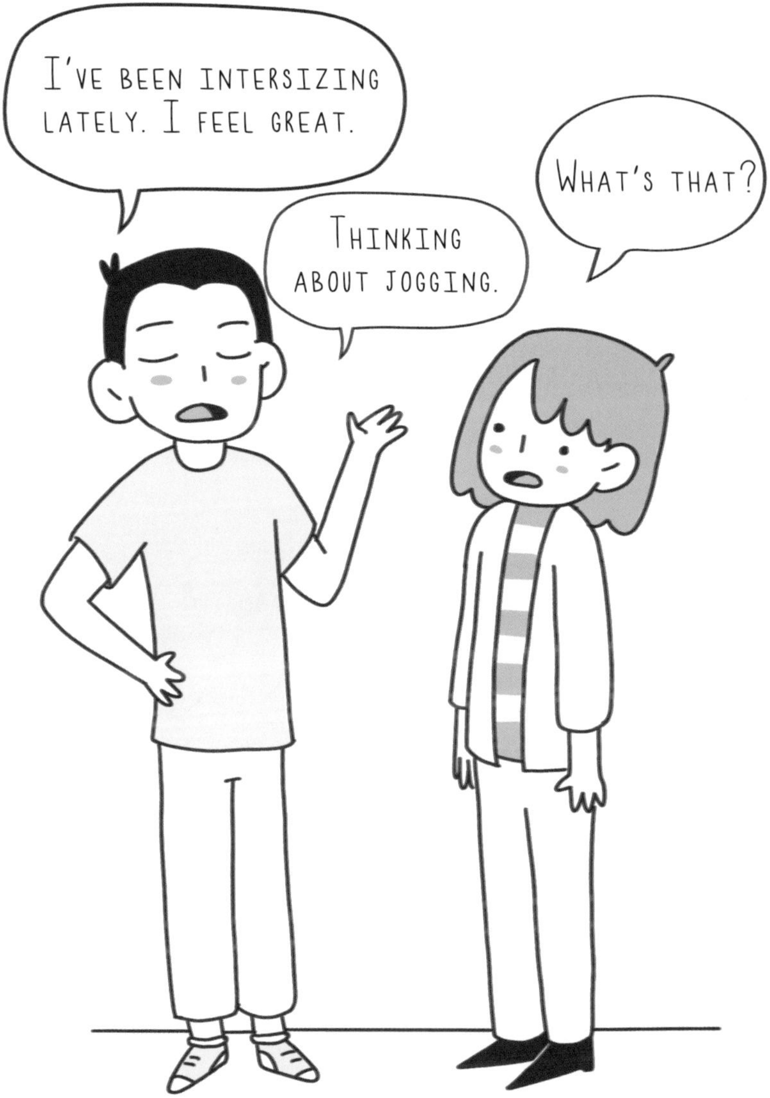
I've been intersizing lately. I feel great.
What's that?
Thinking about jogging.

THERE ARE

MANY WAYS

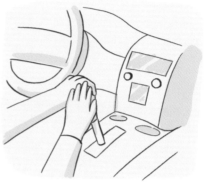

TO SAY

"I LOVE YOU."

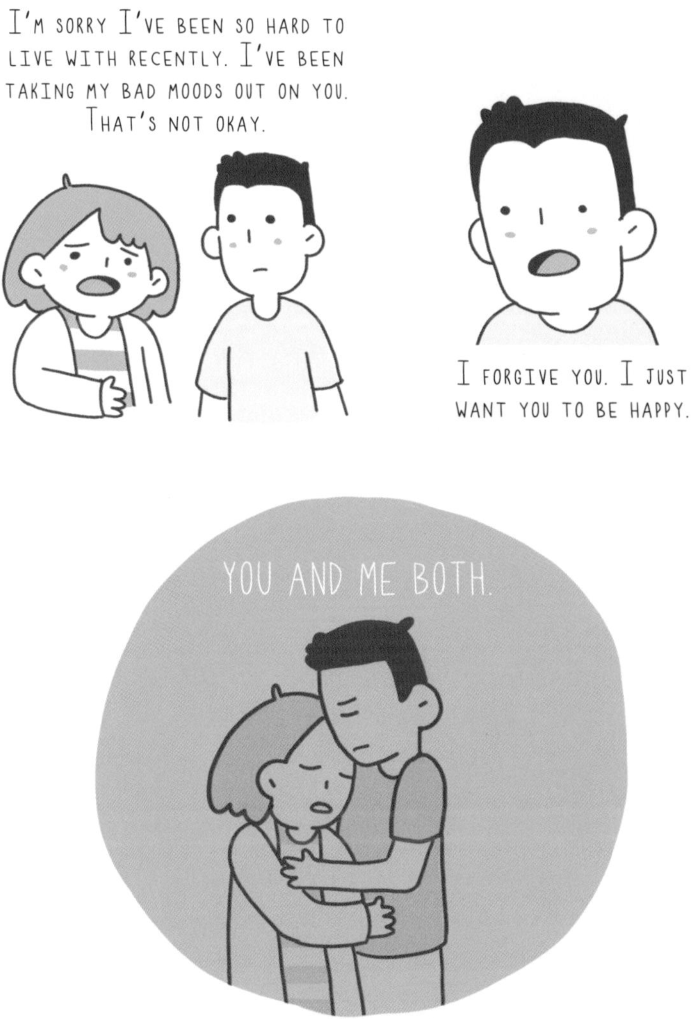
I'M SORRY I'VE BEEN SO HARD TO LIVE WITH RECENTLY. I'VE BEEN TAKING MY BAD MOODS OUT ON YOU. THAT'S NOT OKAY.
I FORGIVE YOU. I JUST WANT YOU TO BE HAPPY.
YOU AND ME BOTH.

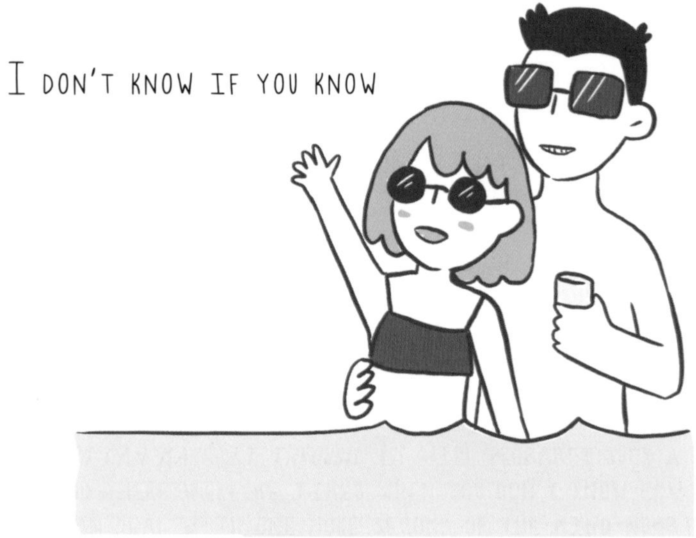
I DON'T KNOW IF YOU KNOW

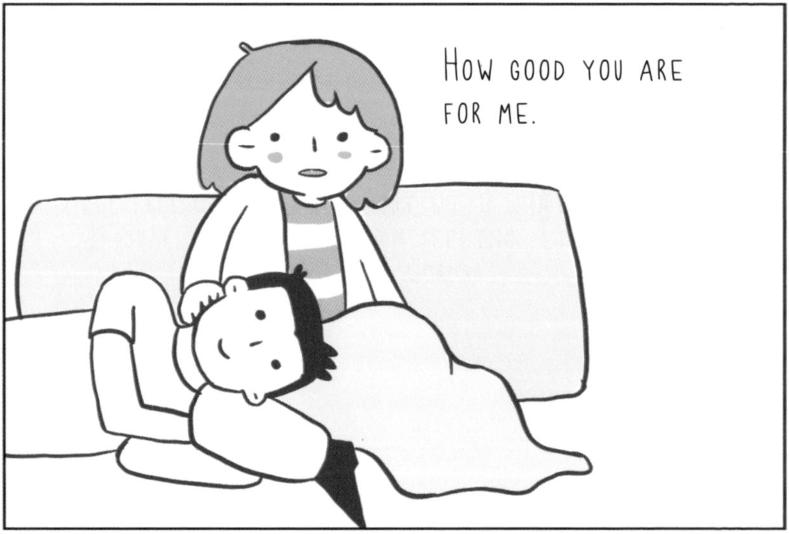
HOW GOOD YOU ARE FOR ME.

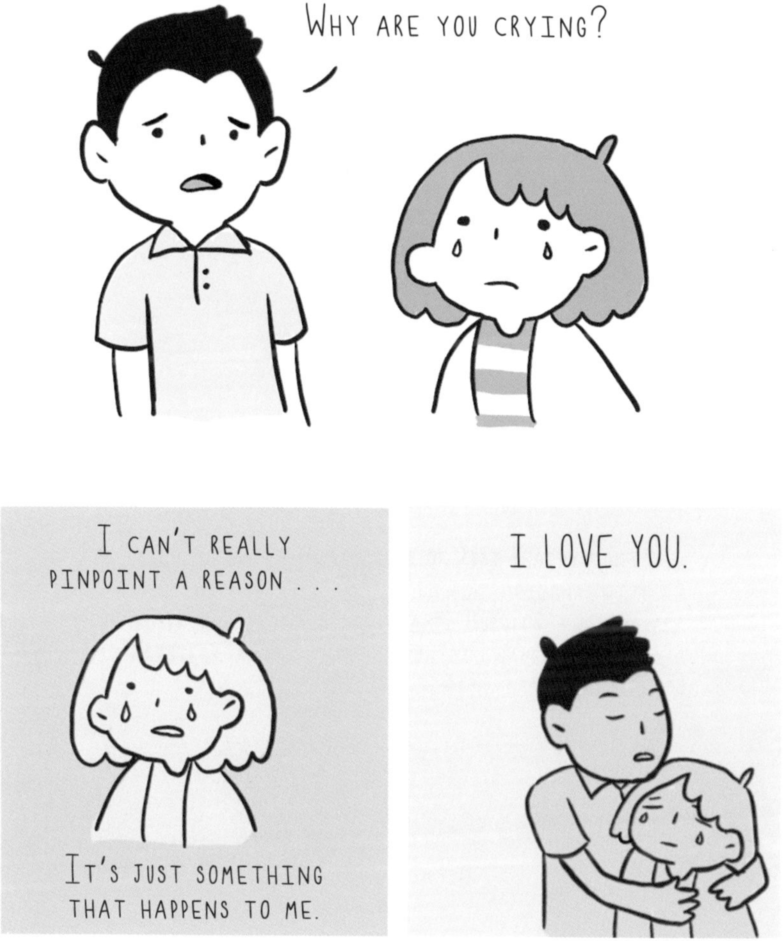
WHY ARE YOU CRYING?
I CAN'T REALLY PINPOINT A REASON . . .
IT'S JUST SOMETHING THAT HAPPENS TO ME.
I LOVE YOU.

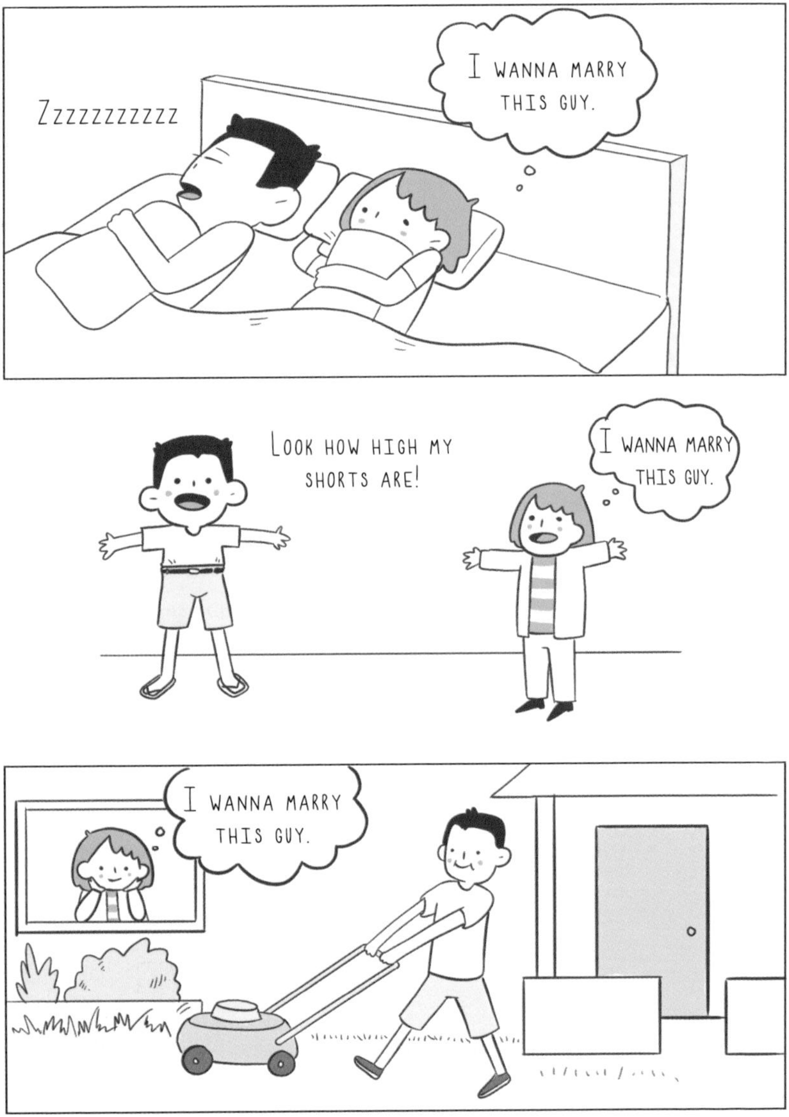
Zzzzzzzzzzz
I WANNA MARRY THIS GUY.
LOOK HOW HIGH MY SHORTS ARE!
I WANNA MARRY THIS GUY.
I WANNA MARRY THIS GUY.

I SAW A SHOOTING STAR . . .

. . . AND REALIZED

I HAD NOTHING TO
WISH FOR.

GROWTH

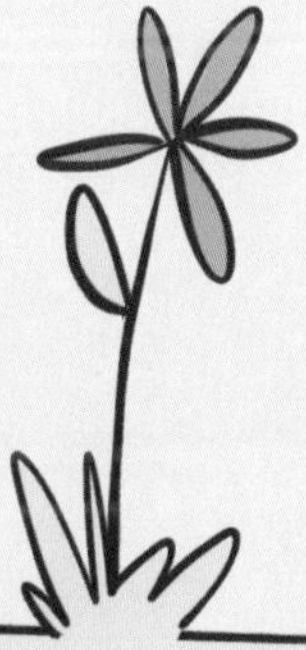

On perseverance:

My artist friend once told me:
"The more you draw, the more you draw!"

Turns out, it's true.

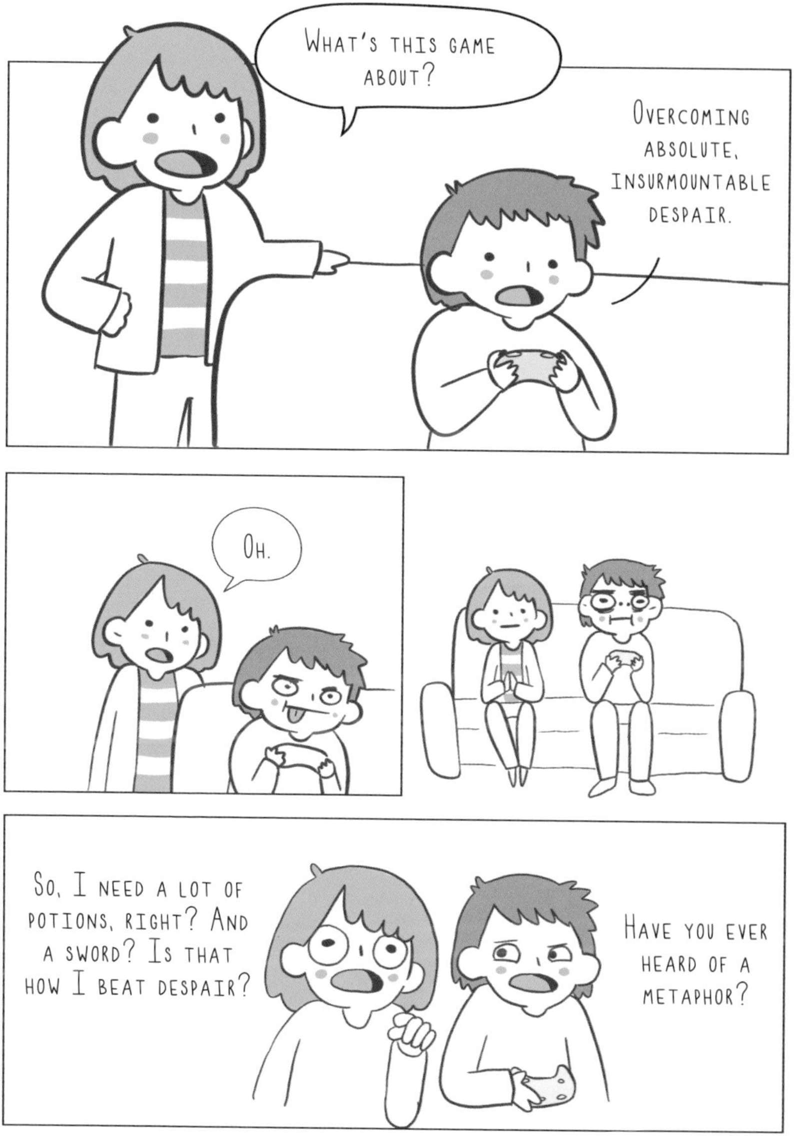
What's this game about?
Overcoming absolute, insurmountable despair.
Oh.
So, I need a lot of potions, right? And a sword? Is that how I beat despair?
Have you ever heard of a metaphor?

I'M SCARED OF ROUTINE.

I DON'T WANT TO BE BORING.

BUT THEN I SEE A SUNSET, WHICH COMES EVERY DAY BUT SOMEHOW ALWAYS SEEMS NEW AND FULL OF HOPE.

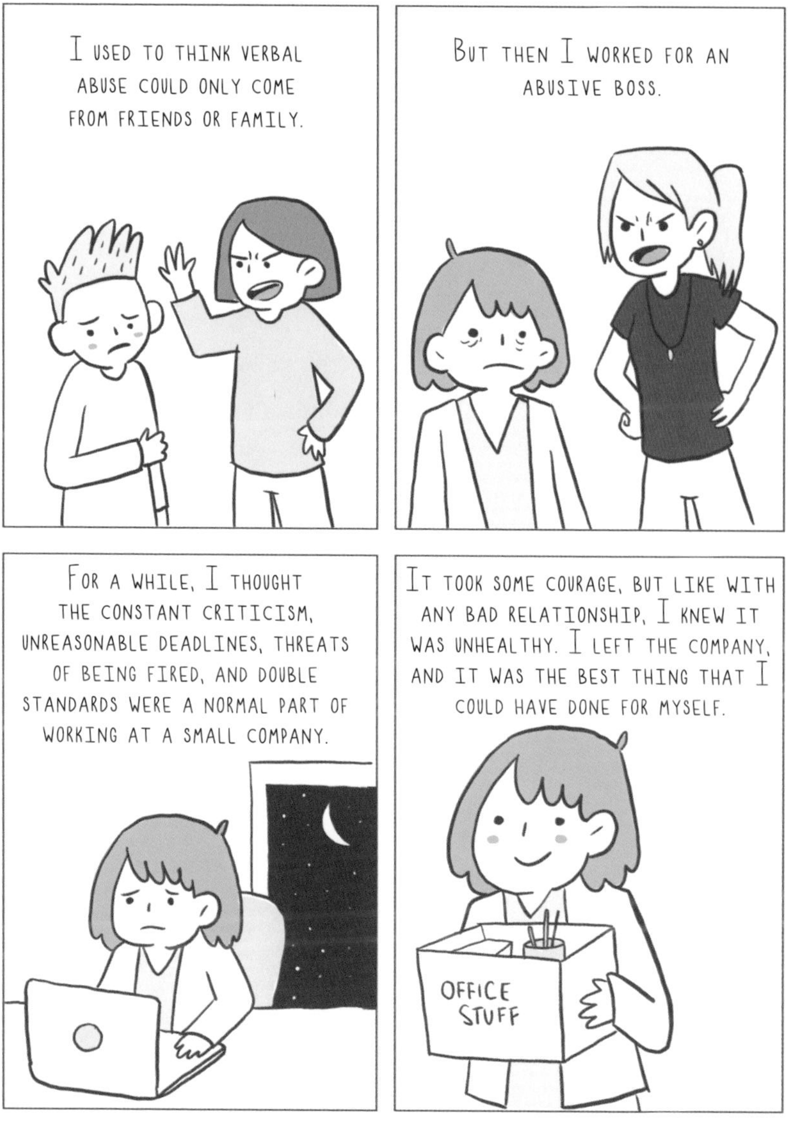
I USED TO THINK VERBAL ABUSE COULD ONLY COME FROM FRIENDS OR FAMILY.
BUT THEN I WORKED FOR AN ABUSIVE BOSS.
FOR A WHILE, I THOUGHT THE CONSTANT CRITICISM, UNREASONABLE DEADLINES, THREATS OF BEING FIRED, AND DOUBLE STANDARDS WERE A NORMAL PART OF WORKING AT A SMALL COMPANY.
IT TOOK SOME COURAGE, BUT LIKE WITH ANY BAD RELATIONSHIP, I KNEW IT WAS UNHEALTHY. I LEFT THE COMPANY, AND IT WAS THE BEST THING THAT I COULD HAVE DONE FOR MYSELF.
OFFICE STUFF

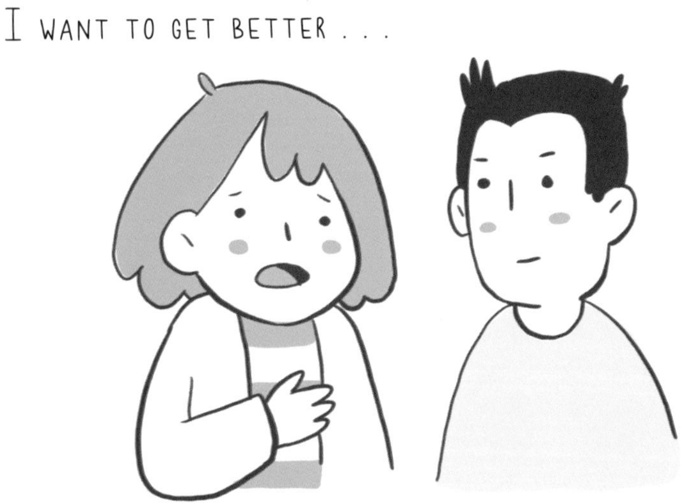
I WANT TO GET BETTER . . .

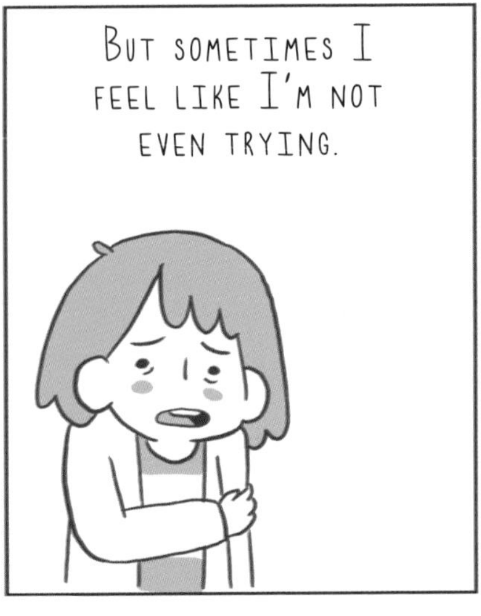
BUT SOMETIMES I FEEL LIKE I'M NOT EVEN TRYING.

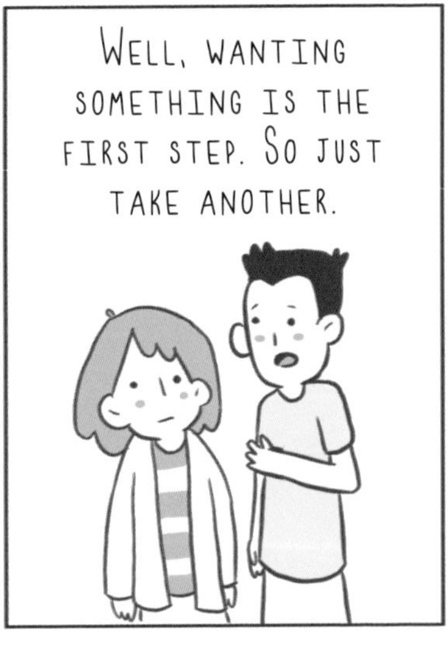
WELL, WANTING SOMETHING IS THE FIRST STEP. SO JUST TAKE ANOTHER.

I WENT FOR A BIKE RIDE FOR THE FIRST TIME IN A WHILE.

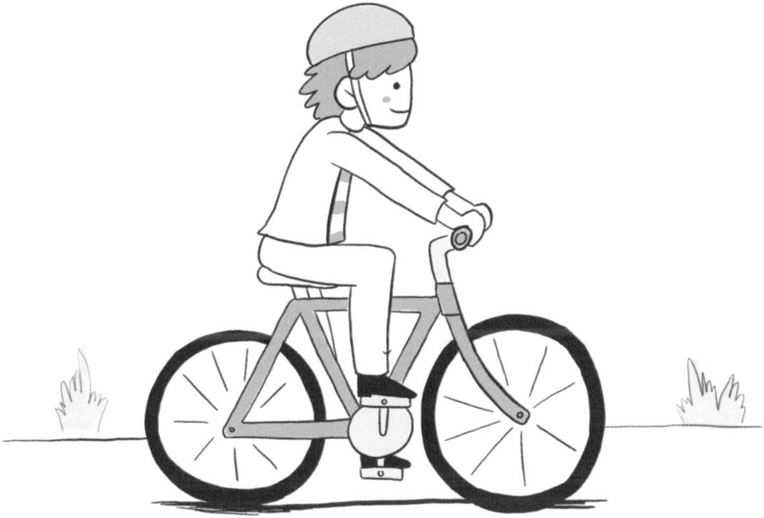

IT WAS SUCH A SMALL THING,

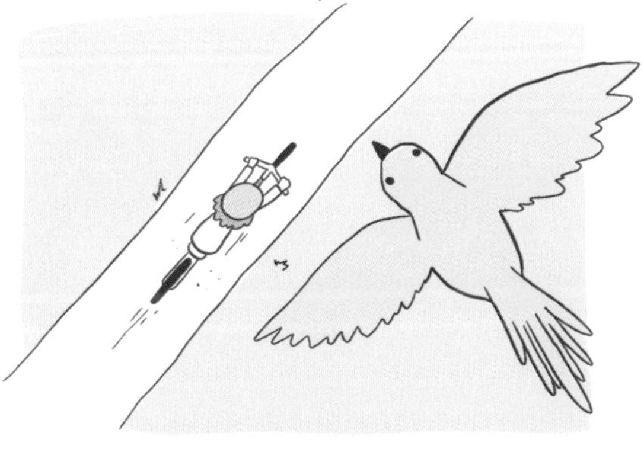

BUT SOMETIMES THE IMPORTANT THINGS ARE.

We all have things we tell ourselves.

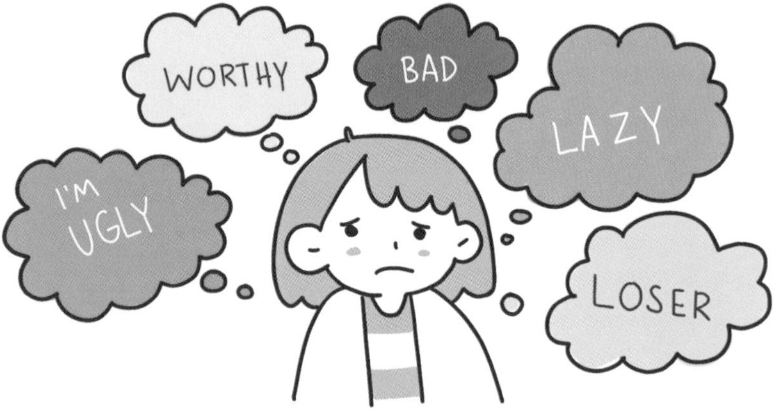
WORTHY
BAD
LAZY
I'M UGLY
LOSER

It's up to us to decide which things are true.

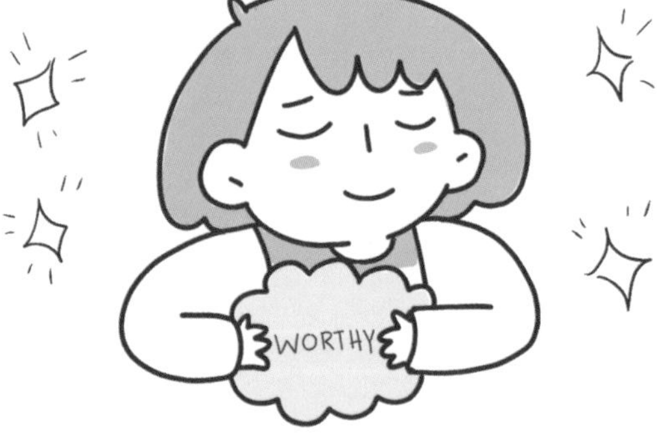
WORTHY

REMEMBER, ONE SMALL RIVER
CARVED OUT THE GRAND CANYON.

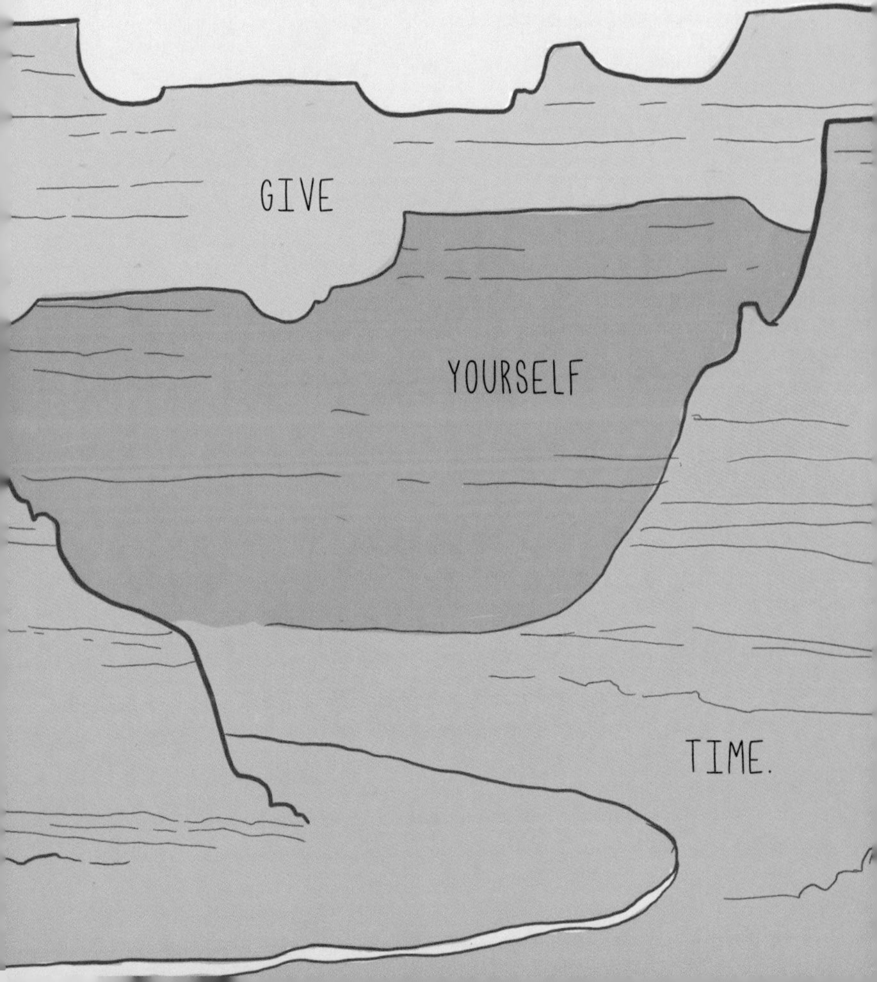
GIVE
YOURSELF
TIME.

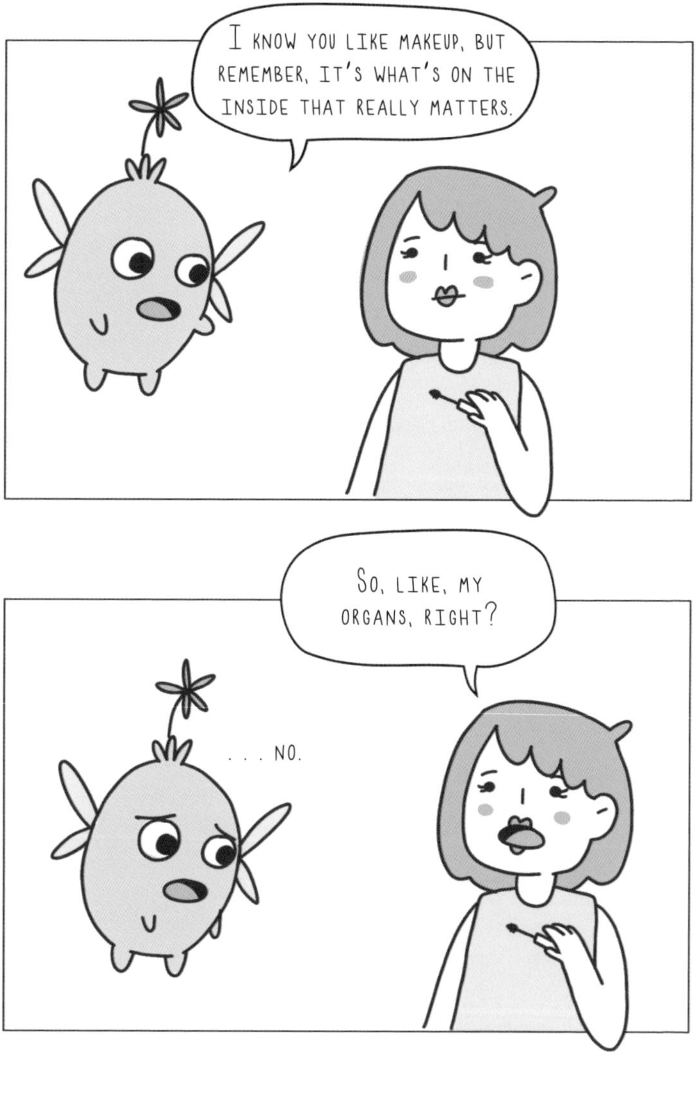
I KNOW YOU LIKE MAKEUP, BUT REMEMBER, IT'S WHAT'S ON THE INSIDE THAT REALLY MATTERS.
SO, LIKE, MY ORGANS, RIGHT?
. . . NO.

SOMETIMES IT'S OKAY TO LIVE FOR SOMETHING BESIDES YOURSELF.

A PET

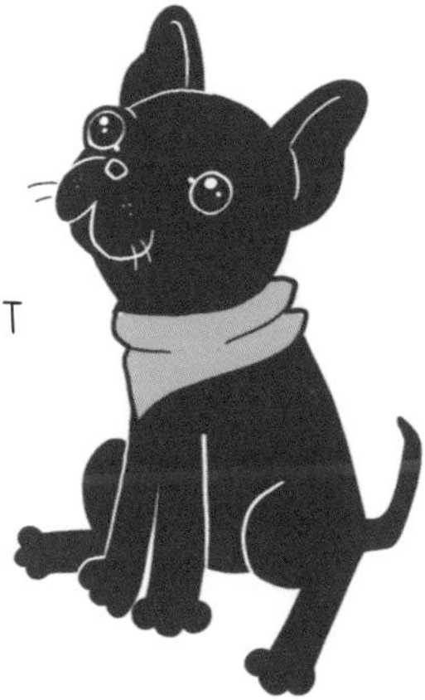

MOM AND DAD

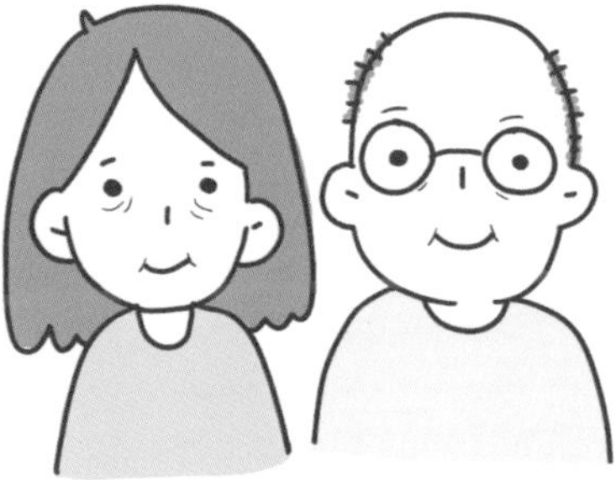

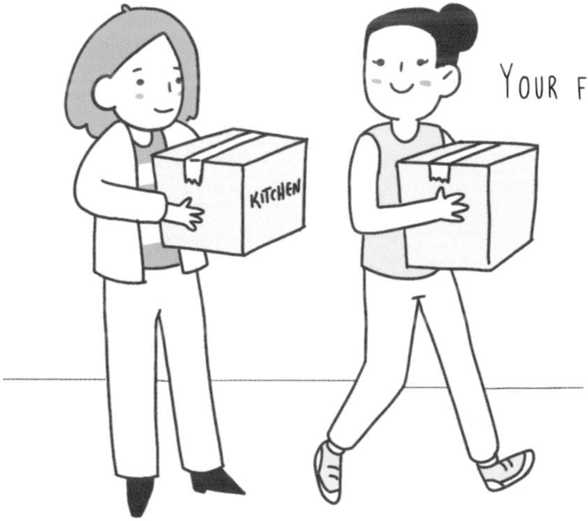
KITCHEN

YOUR FRIENDS

What does recovery look like?

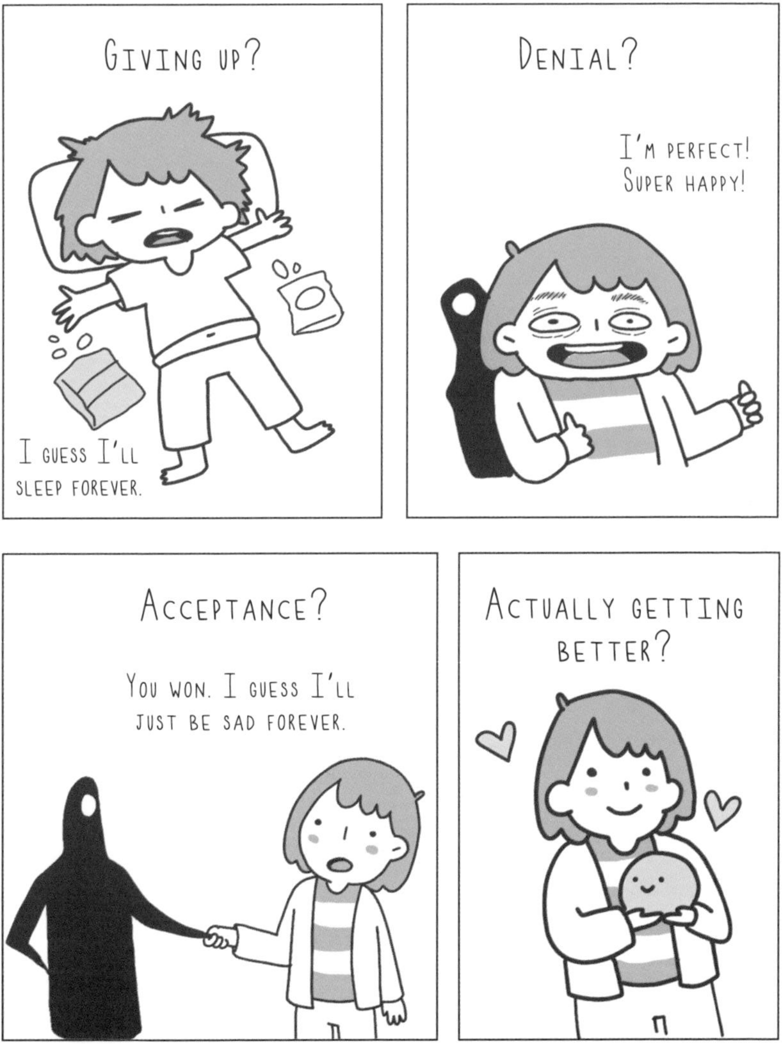
Giving up?
I guess I'll sleep forever.
Denial?
I'm perfect! Super happy!
Acceptance?
You won. I guess I'll just be sad forever.
Actually getting better?

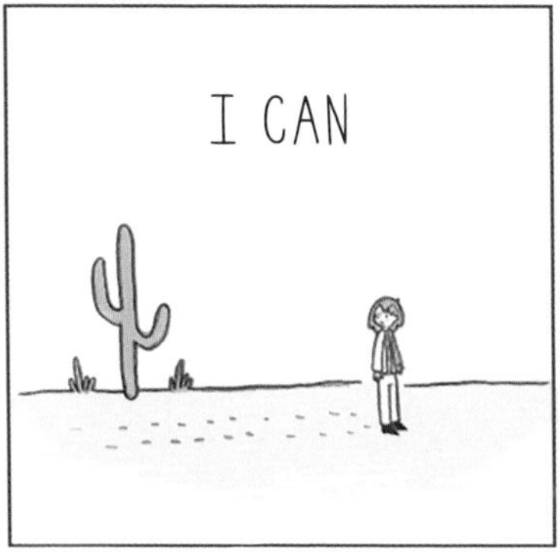
I CAN

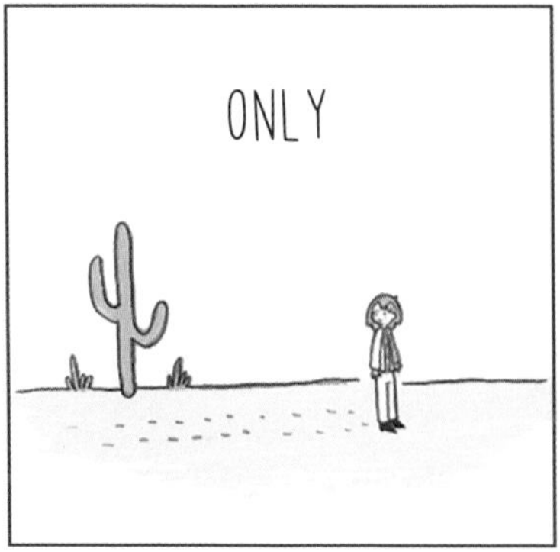
ONLY

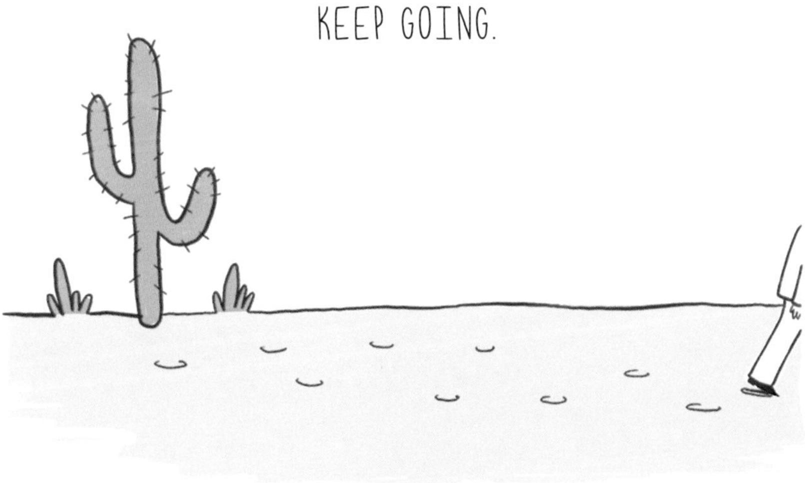
KEEP GOING.

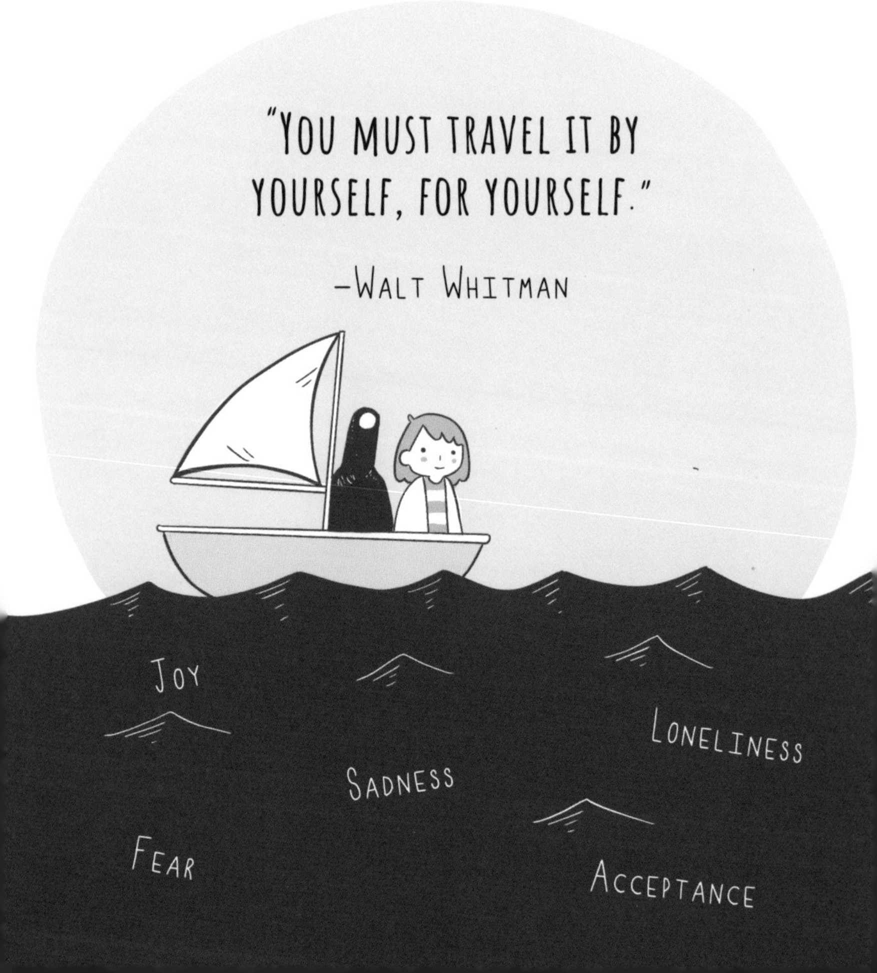
"You must travel it by yourself, for yourself."
–Walt Whitman
Joy
Loneliness
Sadness
Fear
Acceptance

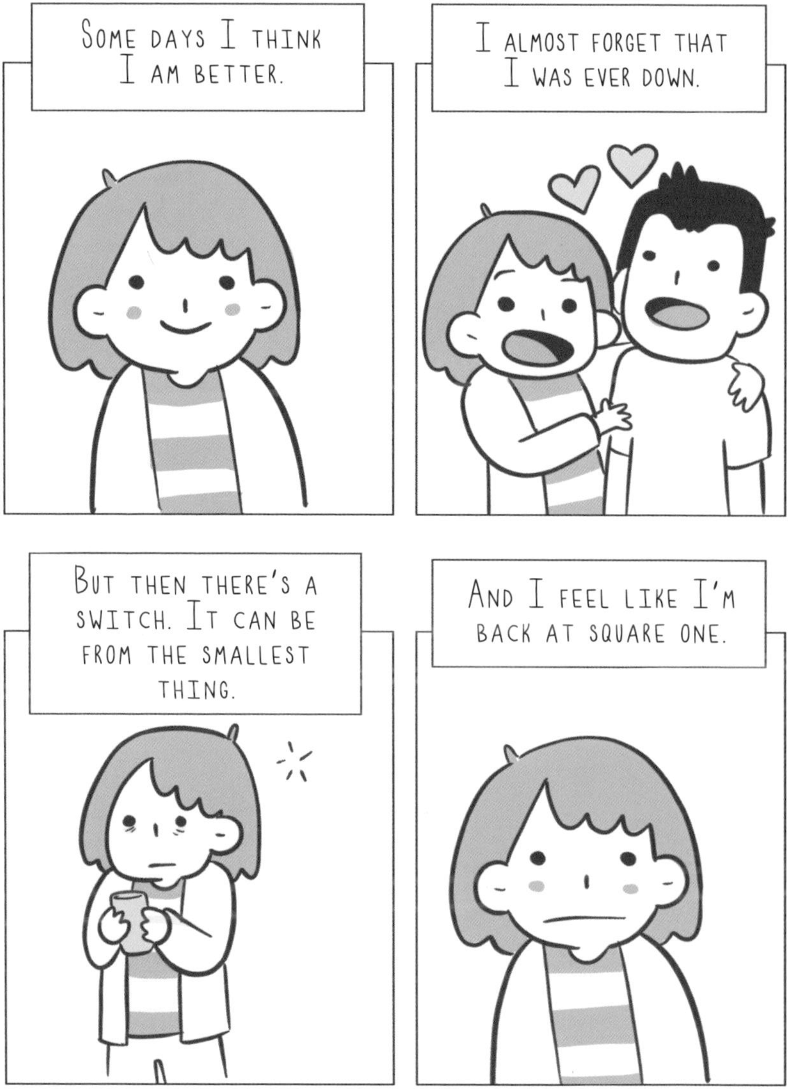
SOME DAYS I THINK I AM BETTER.
I ALMOST FORGET THAT I WAS EVER DOWN.
BUT THEN THERE'S A SWITCH. IT CAN BE FROM THE SMALLEST THING.
AND I FEEL LIKE I'M BACK AT SQUARE ONE.

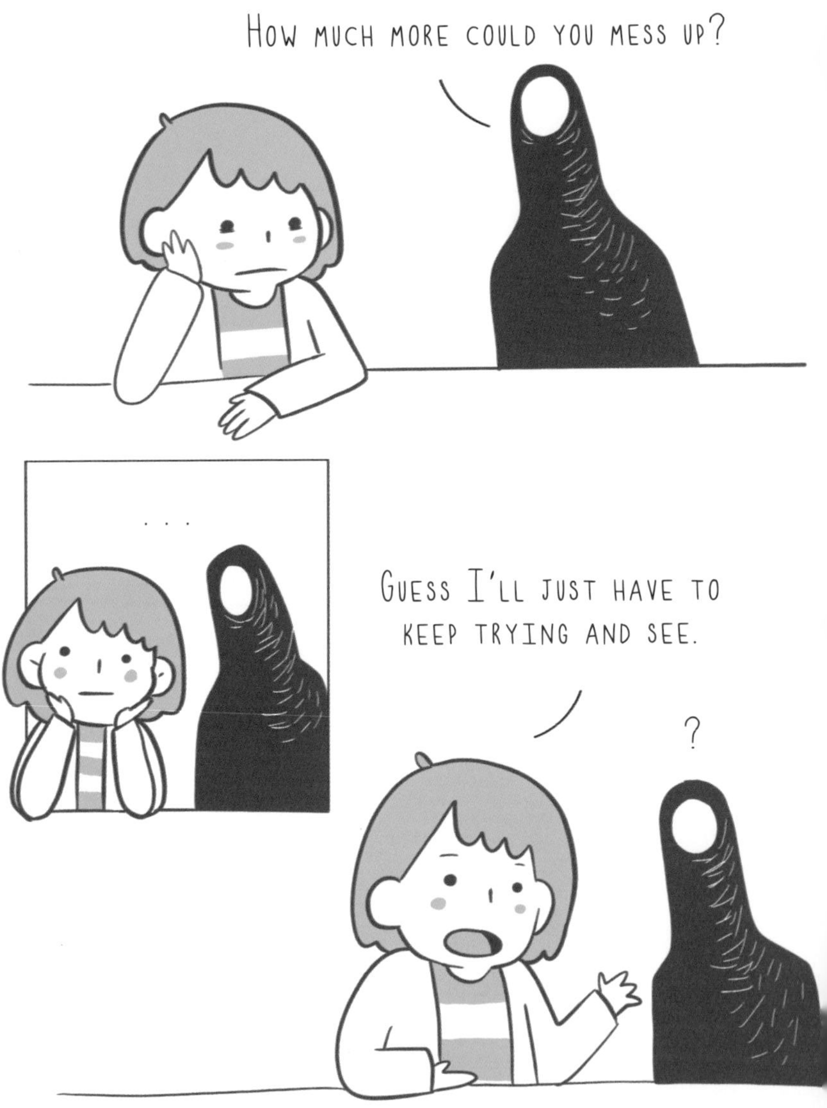
How much more could you mess up?
. . .
Guess I'll just have to keep trying and see.
?

"So far, you've survived 100% of your worst days. You're doing great."

—Norm Kelly

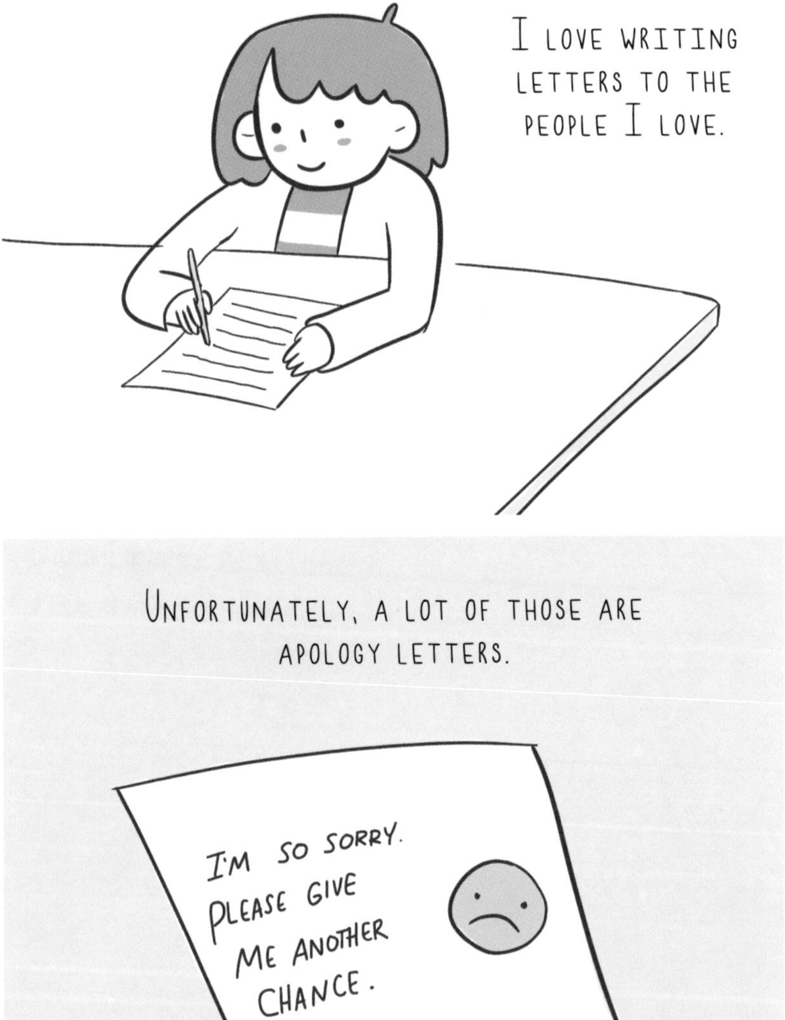
I LOVE WRITING LETTERS TO THE PEOPLE I LOVE.
UNFORTUNATELY, A LOT OF THOSE ARE APOLOGY LETTERS.
I'M SO SORRY. PLEASE GIVE ME ANOTHER CHANCE.

FORMS OF MEDITATION

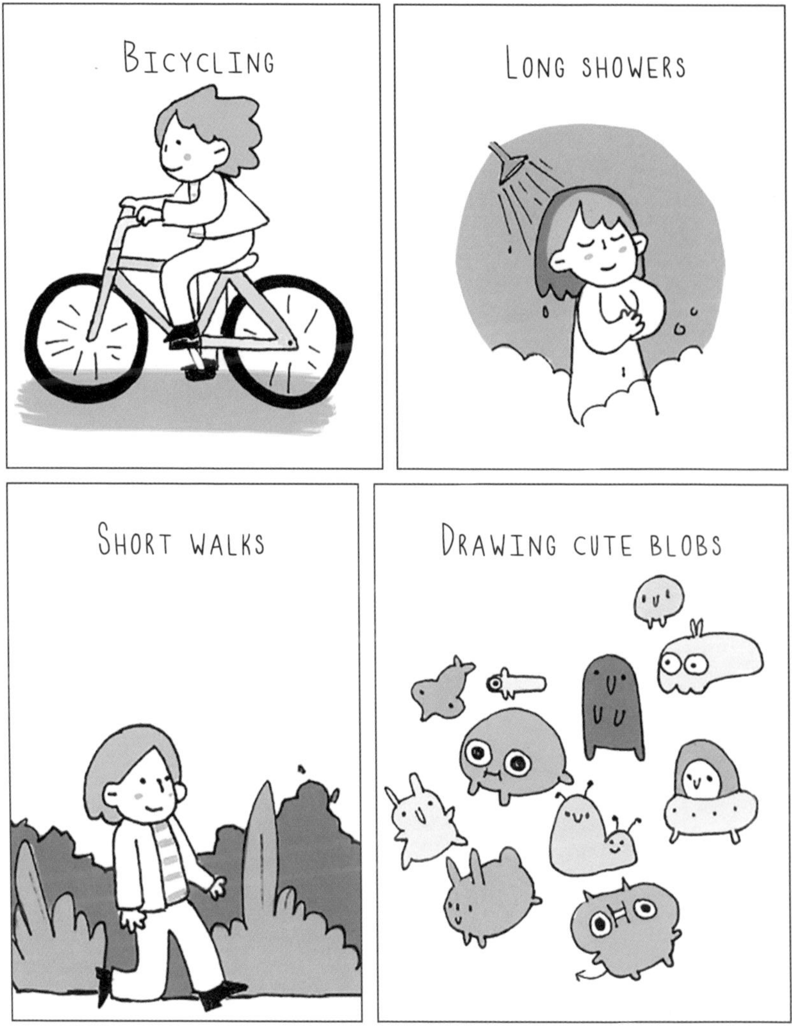
Bicycling
Long showers
Short walks
Drawing cute blobs

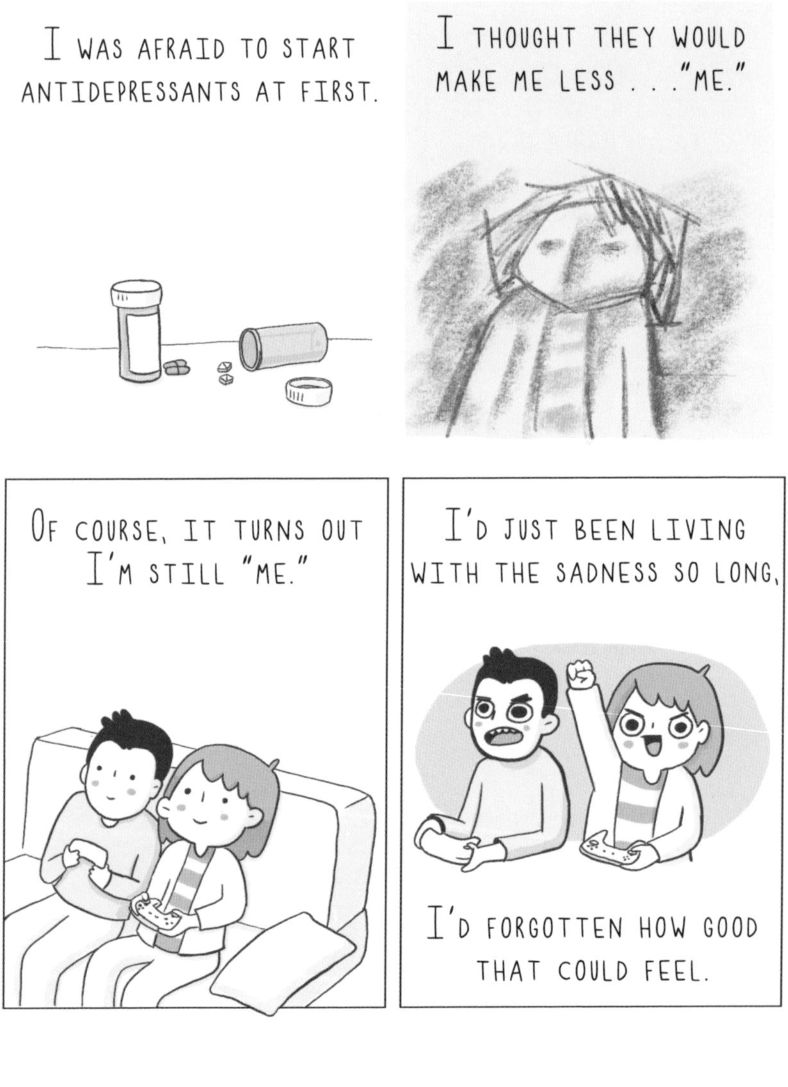
I WAS AFRAID TO START ANTIDEPRESSANTS AT FIRST.
I THOUGHT THEY WOULD MAKE ME LESS . . . "ME."
OF COURSE, IT TURNS OUT I'M STILL "ME."
I'D JUST BEEN LIVING WITH THE SADNESS SO LONG,
I'D FORGOTTEN HOW GOOD THAT COULD FEEL.

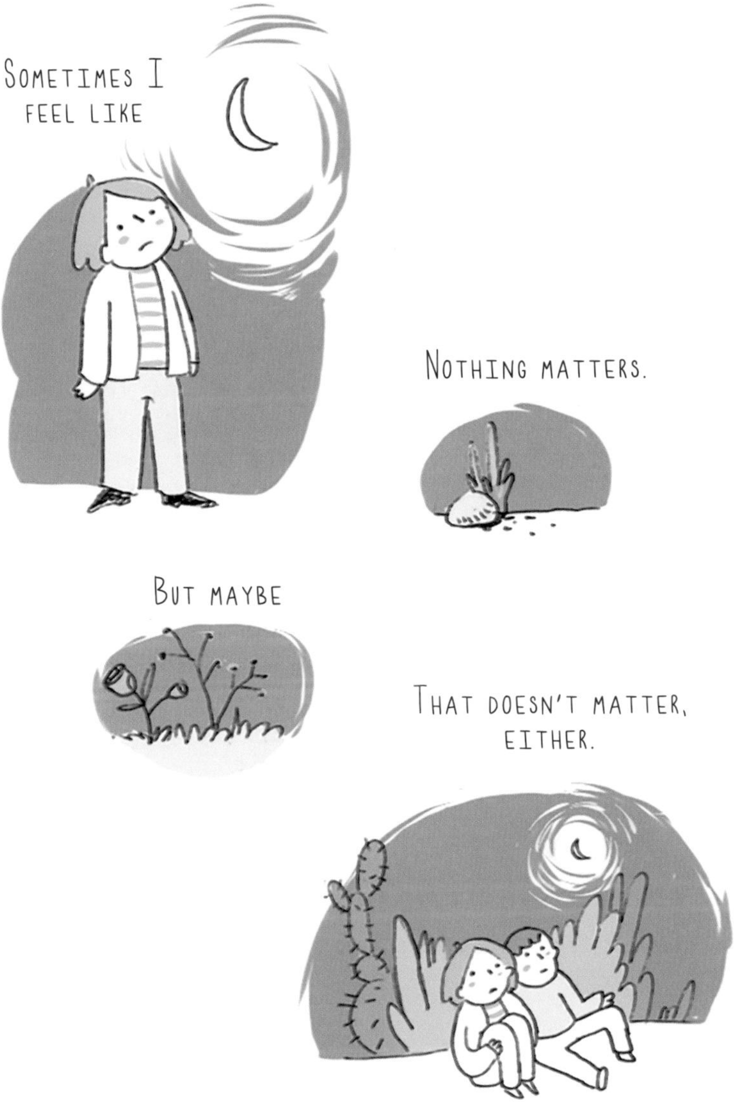
SOMETIMES I FEEL LIKE
NOTHING MATTERS.
BUT MAYBE
THAT DOESN'T MATTER, EITHER.

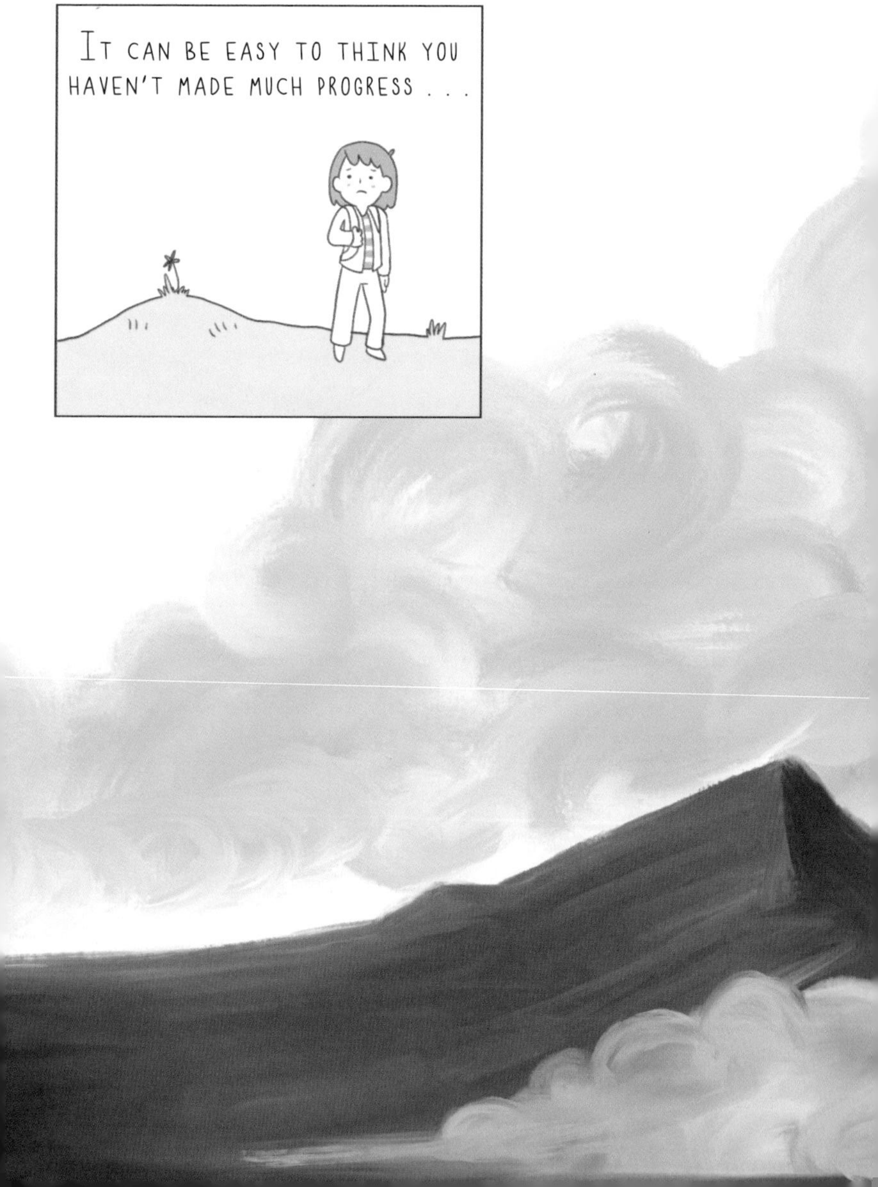
IT CAN BE EASY TO THINK YOU HAVEN'T MADE MUCH PROGRESS . . .

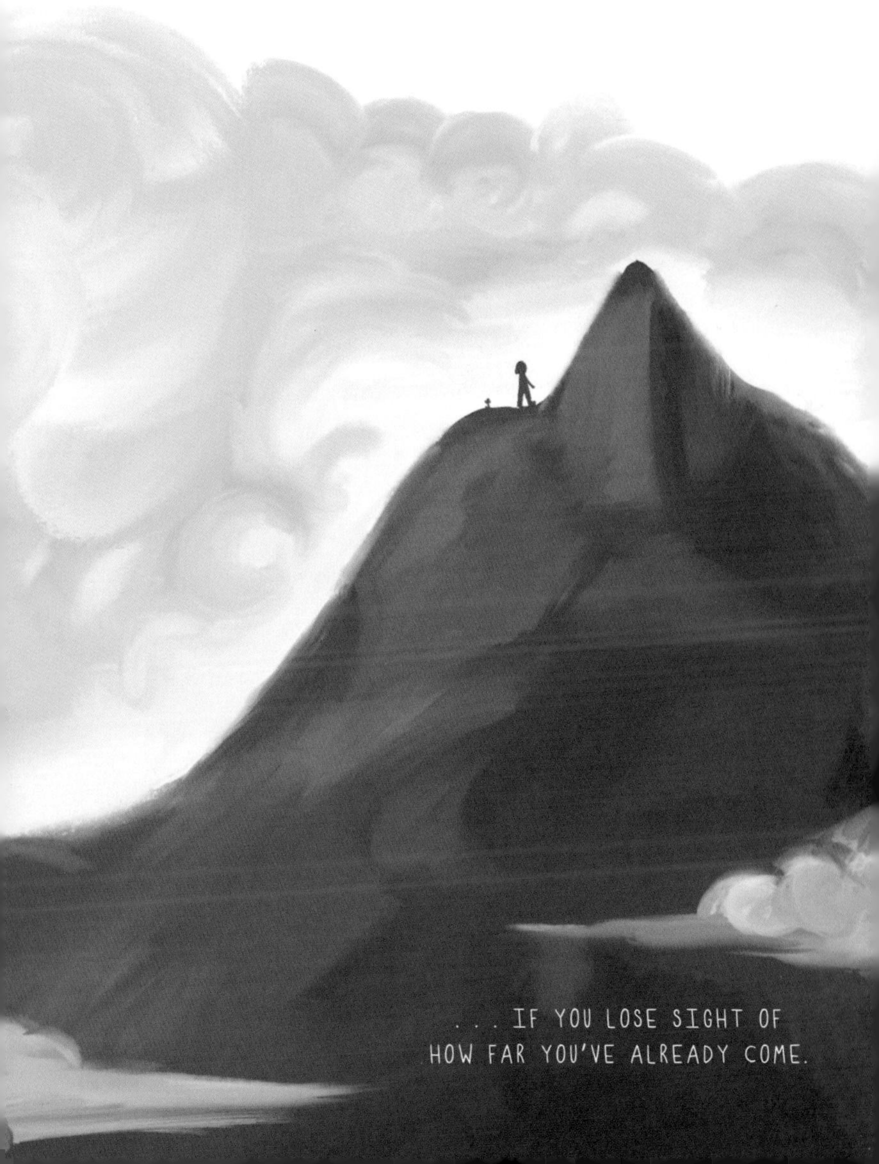
. . . IF YOU LOSE SIGHT OF
HOW FAR YOU'VE ALREADY COME.

Hello there.

Thanks for reading my book. Or just flipping through it and putting it back on the shelf.

I know my comics can be kind of sad, and they aren't that funny, but I hope they spoke to you.

If you are going through depression or anxiety, I would hope this is the one thing you get out of the book:

You can make it through. It will probably suck a lot and there will be times when you don't know how you can deal with one more second of the mind-numbing monotony punctuated with bouts of feeling completely out of control, but you can make it through.

Here, let's try something.

I put some empty boxes on the next page.

Feel free to fill them out with whatever you want. I usually draw how I am feeling. It can even be just words.

There.

Now you have your thoughts in four little boxes.
Sometimes that helps.

Resources

Suicide hotline: 1-800-273-8255

Crisis text line: 741741

Online therapy/coaching
Betterhelp.com
Talkspace.com
Hellopriizm.com

Apps I use for anxiety and addiction
Headspace — meditation app
I am sober — addiction tracking app
Notepad — to write down my thoughts
Procreate — how I draw all my comics

Podcasts
Sleep with me — helps me fall asleep quickly
The hilarious world of depression — conversations with comedians who have depression
Mental health happy hour — conversations about mental health
10% happier podcast — meditation for fidgety skeptics with dan harris

Books that have helped me
The Four Agreements: A Practical Guide to Personal Freedom by Don Miguel Ruiz
The Upward Spiral: Using Neuroscience to Reverse the Course of Depression, One Small Change at a Time by Alex Korb
This Naked Mind: Control Alcohol, Find Freedom, Rediscover Happiness & Change Your Life by Annie Grace
The Power of Now: A Guide to Spiritual Enlightenment by Eckhart Tolle

Acknowledgments

A very special thanks to Dr. Jehangeer Sunderji (my psychiatrist) and Dana Maloney (my therapist).

You both helped me through one of the toughest times in my life and are two of the main reasons this book exists.

Thanks for doing one of the most difficult jobs in the world so brilliantly.

Also, big thanks to Mom, Dad, Luke, Matt, and a plethora of wonderful art teachers who didn't think my drawings were terrible.

More comics @justpeachycomic on Instagram.

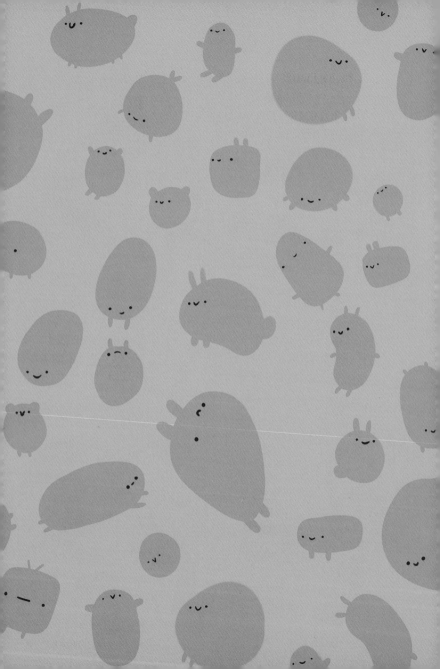

About the Artist

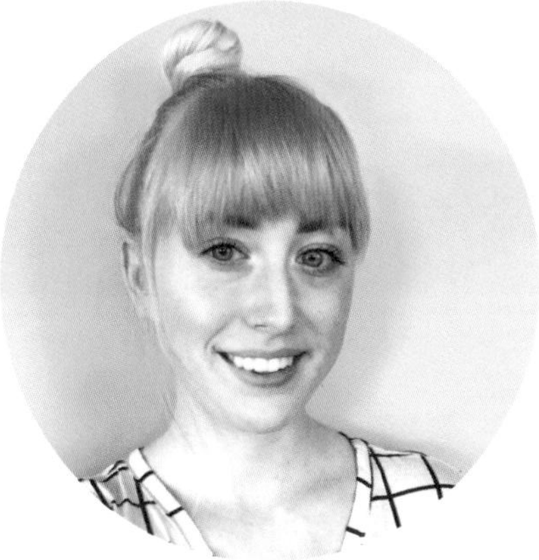

Holly Chisholm is the creator of Just Peachy Comics and is currently living in Phoenix, Arizona, with her boyfriend, Matt; a puppy named Bubbles; two dwarf hamsters; and a cranky cockatiel named Larry.

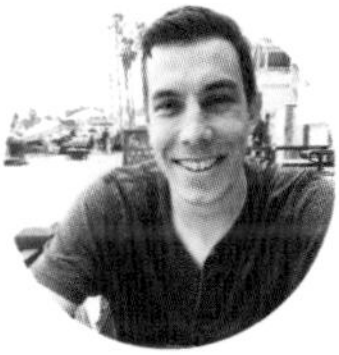

Matt

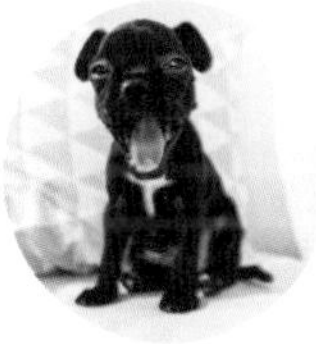

Bubbles

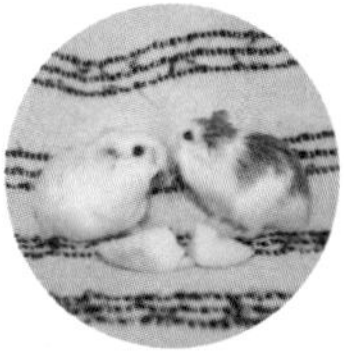

Couscous + Quinoa

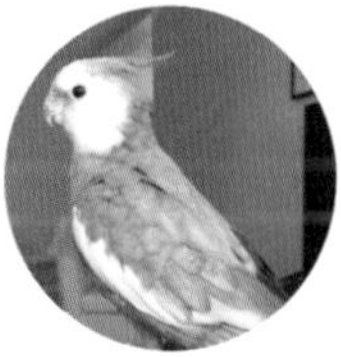

Larry

Copyright © 2019 by Holly Chisholm

All rights reserved. No part of this book may be reproduced in any manner without the express written consent of the publisher, except in the case of brief excerpts in critical reviews or articles. All inquiries should be addressed to Skyhorse Publishing, 307 West 36th Street, 11th Floor, New York, NY 10018.

Skyhorse Publishing books may be purchased in bulk at special discounts for sales promotion, corporate gifts, fund-raising, or educational purposes. Special editions can also be created to specifications. For details, contact the Special Sales Department, Skyhorse Publishing, 307 West 36th Street, 11th Floor, New York, NY 10018 or info@skyhorsepublishing.com.

Skyhorse® and Skyhorse Publishing® are registered trademarks of Skyhorse Publishing, Inc.®, a Delaware corporation.

Visit our website at www.skyhorsepublishing.com.

10 9 8 7 6 5 4

Library of Congress Cataloging-in-Publication Data

Names: Chisholm, Holly, author.
Title: Just peachy : comics about depression, anxiety, love, and finding the
   humor in being sad / Holly Chisholm.
Description: New York, NY : Skyhorse, [2019]
Identifiers: LCCN 2018045299| ISBN 9781510742000 (hardback) | ISBN
   9781510742048 (ebook)
Subjects: LCSH: Creative writing--Therapeutic use. | Depression,
   Mental--Humor. | BISAC: SELF-HELP / Depression. | HUMOR / General.
Classification: LCC RC489.W75 C48 2019 | DDC 616.89/1663--dc23 LC record available at https://lccn.loc.gov/2018045299

Cover design and illustration by Holly Chisholm

Print ISBN: 978-1-5107-4200-0
Ebook ISBN: 978-1-5107-4204-8

Printed in China